By Alison Lurie

FICTION

Love and Friendship
The Nowhere City
Imaginary Friends
Real People
The War Between the Tates
Only Children
Foreign Affairs
The Truth About Lorin Jones
Women and Ghosts
The Last Resort

NONFICTION

V. R. Lang: A Memoir
The Language of Clothes
Don't Tell the Grown-Ups

FOR CHILDREN

Clever Gretchen and Other Forgotten Folk Tales
The Heavenly Zoo
Fabulous Beasts

EDITED BY ALISON LURIE

The Oxford Book of Modern Fairy Tales

Don't Tell the Grown-Ups

THE SUBVERSIVE POWER
OF CHILDREN'S LITERATURE

Alison Lurie

Little, Brown and Company

BOSTON   NEW YORK   TORONTO   LONDON

Originally published in hardcover by Little, Brown and Company, 1990
First Back Bay paperback edition, 1998

Some of these essays have appeared, in a different form and under different titles, in the following publications. They are reprinted by permission.

Children's Literature: "Back to Pooh Corner," "Ford Madox Ford's Fairy Tales"

Harper's Magazine: "Vulgar, Coarse and Grotesque"

Ms.: "Lost Women: Beatrix Potter"

New York Review of Books: "The Boy Who Couldn't Grow Up," "Braking for Elves," "Fairy Tale Liberation," "The Fate of the Munchkins," "Happy Endings," "Life's Greatest Hits," "The Power of Smokey," "Riding the Wave of the Future," "The Round Table in Ruins," " A Tale of Terror," "Underground Genius," "Witches and Fairies: Fitzgerald to Updike," "The World of the Pied Piper"

New York Times Book Review: "Beatrix Potter in Paper," "The Juniper Tree and Other Tales from Grimm," "Now We Are Fifty"

Signet Classics: Introduction to *Peter Pan*

LIBRARY OF CONGRESS CATALOGING-IN-PUBLICATION DATA

Lurie, Alison.
    Don't tell the grown-ups : subversive children's literature /
Alison Lurie. — 1st ed.
        p.   cm.
    Includes bibliographical references.
    ISBN 0-316-53722-5 (hc) / 0-316-24625-5 (pb)
    1. Children's literature, English — History and criticism.
2. Children — Books and reading.   I. Title.
PR990.L8   1990
820.9'9282 — dc20   89-14567

10 9 8 7 6 5 4 3 2 1

MV-NY

For Doris

Contents

Foreword

There exists in our world an unusual, partly savage tribe, ancient and widely distributed, yet until recently little studied by anthropologists or historians. All of us were at one time members of this tribe: we knew its customs, manners, and rituals, its folklore and sacred texts. I refer, of course, to children.

The sacred texts of childhood, however, are not always the ones adults recommend, as I discovered very early. Soon after I began going to the library, I realized that there were two sorts of books on its shelves. The first kind, the great majority, told me what grown-ups had decided I ought to know or believe about the world. Many of these books were practical: they wanted me to understand how the automobile worked, or who George Washington was. Also, and not just incidentally, they wanted me to admire both automobiles and the Father of Our Country; you didn't hear much about the mothers of our country in those days.

Along with these improving books there were also some that hoped to teach me manners or morals or both. These books had no Dewey decimal numbers on their spines, and their lessons came disguised as stories. They were about children or bunny rabbits or little engines who had problems or faults and got into difficult situations, sometimes comic and sometimes serious. But in the end they were always saved by some wise, helpful older person or rabbit or engine.

The protagonists of these books, that is, learned to depend on authority for help and advice. They also learned to be hardworking, responsible, and practical; to stay on the track and be content with their lot in life. They learned, in other words, to be more like respectable grown-ups. It was the same message I and my friends heard every day: Sit up straight, dear. Don't go too far into the woods. Say thank you to Aunt Etta. Come along, stop daydreaming and fill in your workbook. Now, darling, you mustn't make up stories.

But there was another sort of children's literature, I discovered. Some of these books, like *Tom Sawyer, Little Women, Peter Pan,* and *Alice's Adventures in Wonderland,* were on the shelves of the library; others, like *The Wizard of Oz* and the Nancy Drew series, had been judged unworthy and had to be bought in shops or borrowed from friends. These were the sacred texts of childhood, whose authors had not forgotten what it was like to be a child. To read them was to feel a shock of recognition, a rush of liberating energy.

These books, and others like them, recommended — even celebrated — daydreaming, disobedience, answering back, running away from home, and concealing one's private thoughts and feelings from unsympathetic grown-ups. They overturned adult pretensions and made fun of adult institutions, including school and family. In a word, they were subversive, just like many of the rhymes and jokes and games I learned on the school playground.

It is a long while since I was a child, but I don't think the situation has changed very much. In every era, including the present one, run-of-the-mill children's literature tends to support the status quo. The books that win prizes for stylistic or artistic excellence often — though not always — belong to this category; and when they do, they are at best only politely tolerated by children.

*

I AM SOMETIMES asked why anyone who is not a teacher
or a librarian or the parent of little kids should concern herself
with children's books and folklore. I know the standard answers: that many famous writers have written for children,
and that the great children's books are also great literature;
that these books and tales are an important source of archetype and symbol, and that they can help us to understand the
structure and functions of the novel.

All this is true. But I think we should also take children's
literature seriously because it is sometimes subversive: because its values are not always those of the conventional adult
world. Of course, in a sense much great literature is subversive, since its very existence implies that what matters
is art, imagination, and truth. In what we call the real world,
on the other hand, what usually counts is money, power, and
public success.

The great subversive works of children's literature suggest that there are other views of human life besides those
of the shopping mall and the corporation. They mock current
assumptions and express the imaginative, unconventional,
noncommercial view of the world in its simplest and purest
form. They appeal to the imaginative, questioning, rebellious
child within all of us, renew our instinctive energy, and act
as a force for change. This is why such literature is worthy
of our attention and will endure long after more conventional
tales have been forgotten.

THE WRITERS discussed in this book are a mixed bag. Their
work ranges from simple verses and drawings for small children to lengthy sagas. What they have in common is, first,
that most of them are British. Why so much great children's
literature should have been written in England is still a matter

for discussion. Perhaps the phenomenon can be traced back to the Romantic movement and the value put on childhood by writers like Blake and Wordsworth, which suggested to men and women of genius that writing for and about children was a serious and worthy occupation. Even today, this tradition continues, and British authors do not make the sort of apology for their work ("It's only a children's book, of course") that is often heard elsewhere.

More important, all the writers discussed here tended to overturn rather than uphold the conventional values of their period or background. Some of them, like E. Nesbit, Frances Hodgson Burnett, and William Mayne, popularized new and controversial political, social, or psychological ideas. Some, like Beatrix Potter, A. A. Milne, and Richard Adams, portrayed a society of actual or imaginary animals as an ironic or ideal version of reality. Some, like Kate Greenaway, J.R.R. Tolkien, and T. H. White, created imaginary worlds that were by implication superior to the one that surrounded them. Others, like Mrs. Clifford and Ford Madox Ford, used the form of the children's story to explore their private dreams and nightmares. Of course, these aims are not exclusive: James Barrie's *Peter Pan*, for instance, is at one and the same time a personal fantasy, a satirical look at contemporary domestic life, and a manifesto for the claims of imagination against rationality.

The chapters on folklore have a similar underlying theme. They investigate the ways in which fairy tales, legends, rhymes, jokes, and superstitions can be used to express whatever is muted, suppressed, or compromised in mainstream culture. For example, folklore may tell us that children already know some of the secrets of adult life of which they are supposed to be ignorant; or it may suggest that people we usually despise and overlook have unsuspected powers.

*

AN INTERESTING question is, what — besides intention — makes a particular story a "children's book"? With the exception of picture books for toddlers, these works are not necessarily shorter or simpler than so-called adult fiction, and they are surely not less well written. The heroes and heroines of these tales, it is true, are often children: but then so are the protagonists of Henry James's *What Maisie Knew* and Toni Morrison's *The Bluest Eye*. Yet the barrier between children's books and adult fiction remains; editors, critics, and readers seem to have little trouble in assigning a given work to one category or the other.

In classic children's fiction a pastoral convention is maintained. It is assumed that the world of childhood is simpler and more natural than that of adults, and that children, though they may have faults, are essentially good or at least capable of becoming so. The transformation of selfish, whiny, disagreeable Mary and hysterical, demanding Colin in Frances Hodgson Burnett's *The Secret Garden* is a paradigm. Of course, there are often unpleasant minor juvenile characters who give the protagonist a lot of trouble and are defeated or evaded rather than reeducated. But on occasion even the angry bully and the lying sneak can be reformed and forgiven. Richard Hughes's *A High Wind in Jamaica*, though most of its characters are children, never appears on lists of recommended juvenile fiction; not so much because of the elaborations of its diction (which is no more complex than that of, say, *Treasure Island*), but because in it children are irretrievably damaged and corrupted.

Adults in most children's books, on the other hand, are usually stuck with their characters and incapable of alteration or growth. If they are really unpleasant, the only thing that can rescue them is the natural goodness of a child. Here again Mrs. Burnett provides the classic example, in *Little Lord*

Fauntleroy. (Scrooge's somewhat similar change of heart in Dickens's *A Christmas Carol,* however, is due mainly to regret for his past and terror of the future. This is one of the things that make the book a family rather than a juvenile romance; another is the helpless passivity of the principal child character, Tiny Tim.)

Of the three principal preoccupations of adult fiction — sex, money, and death — the first is absent from classic children's literature and the other two either absent or much muted. Love in these stories may be intense, but it is romantic rather than sensual, at least overtly. Peter Pan passionately desires Wendy, but what he wants is for her to be his mother.

Money is a motive in children's literature, in the sense that many stories deal with a search for treasure of some sort. These quests, unlike real-life ones, are almost always successful, though occasionally what is found in the end is some form of family happiness, which is declared by the author and the characters to be a "real treasure." Simple economic survival, however, is almost never the problem; what is sought, rather, is a magical (sometimes literally magical) surplus of wealth.

Death, which was a common theme in nineteenth-century fiction for children, was almost banished during the first half of this century. Since then it has begun to reappear; the breakthrough book was E. B. White's *Charlotte's Web.* Today not only animals but people die, notably in the sort of books that get awards and are recommended by librarians and psychologists for children who have lost a relative. But even today the characters who die tend to be of another generation; the protagonist and his or her friends survive.

Though there are some interesting exceptions, even the most subversive of contemporary children's books usually follow these conventions. They portray an ideal world of perfectible beings, free of the necessity for survival and reproduction: not only a pastoral but a paradisal universe — for without sex and death, humans may become as angels. The romantic child, trailing clouds of glory, is not as far off as we might think.

MANY PEOPLE deserve my thanks for their contributions to this book. I am most grateful to Barbara Epstein of the *New York Review of Books,* who first encouraged me to write about children's literature and published the original versions of many of these essays, and to Francelia Butler, the founder of the journal *Children's Literature,* where others appeared.

I should like to thank the students in my lecture course at Cornell University, who were the first to hear many of these ideas and whose comments were often original and interesting. My special thanks are due to the graduate students who have taught and lectured in this course — Kathryn Aal, Melissa Bank, Diana Chlebek, Susan Laird, Beth Lordan, Mary Ann Rishel, Roberta Valente, and Katherine Wright — for their intelligent and imaginative understanding of children's literature and folklore.

I am grateful also to Heather Alexander, my undergraduate research assistant, and to Phyllis Molock, who uncomplainingly and accurately typed many faded and torn clippings into the computer.

Finally, I should like to thank my sons, John, Jeremy, and Joshua Bishop, who provided firsthand experience of how children react to books; and also Jane Gardam and Shel Silverstein, who in very different ways know from the inside what it is like to be the author of subversive children's literature.

Ithaca, New York
May 1989

DON'T TELL THE GROWN-UPS

1

Subversive Children's Literature

Imagine an ideal suburban or small-town elementary school yard at recess. Sunshine, trees, swings; children playing tag or jumping rope — a scene of simplicity and innocence. Come nearer; what are those nice little girls chanting as they turn the rope?

> "Fudge, fudge, tell the judge,
> Mama has a baby.
> It's a boy, full of joy,
> Papa's going crazy.
> Wrap it up in toilet paper,
> Send it down the elevator."

Soon the school bell will sound and the children will file into assembly. Gazing up at the American flag on the stage, they will lift their young voices in patriotic song:

> "My country's tired of me,
> I'm going to Germany,
> To see the king.
> His name is Donald Duck,
> He drives a garbage truck,
> He taught me how to – – – –.
> Let freedom ring."

Adults who have forgotten what childhood is really like may be shocked by these verses; but anyone who has recently read *Tom Sawyer, Alice's Adventures in Wonderland,* or any of a number of other classics should not be surprised. Most of the great works of juvenile literature are subversive in one way or another: they express ideas and emotions not generally approved of or even recognized at the time; they make fun of honored figures and piously held beliefs; and they view social pretenses with clear-eyed directness, remarking — as in Andersen's famous tale — that the emperor has no clothes.

Mark Twain's *Tom Sawyer,* for instance, is not the kind of story contemporary authorities recommended for children. It was in fact written in irritable reaction against what Twain described as "goody-goody boys' books" — the improving tales that were distributed in tremendous numbers by religious and educational institutions in nineteenth-century America. The standard plot of such works was that known to folklorists as "Kind and Unkind." It is perhaps most familiar to us from Hogarth's series of prints depicting the lives of the Good and Bad Apprentices, the former of whom practices every virtue and rises to riches and honor, while his lazy, thieving companion dies penniless.

In *Tom Sawyer* Twain deliberately turned this plot on its head. Tom lies, steals, swears, smokes tobacco, plays hooky, and wins a Sunday school prize by fraud. He sneaks out of his house at night and runs away for days, driving his aunt Polly almost to despair. He ends up with a small fortune in gold, the admiration of the whole town, and the love of Becky Thatcher — while his goody-goody brother Sid is last seen being literally kicked and cuffed out the door.

Twain's portrait of his hometown, Hannibal, Missouri (which appears in the book as St. Petersburg), is equally seditious. Its adult citizens are shown as petty, credulous, and overawed by wealth, and their most respected local institutions are empty shams. The Temperance Tavern shelters thieves and outlaws, and sells whiskey in its back room. Church is a place of excruciating weekly boredom where "the choir always tittered and whispered all through service"[1] and the entire congregation is delighted when the sermon is disrupted by a yelping dog. School is even worse: the teacher is a small-time tyrant who shames and beats his students while laboriously training the more docile ones to recite bad poetry and even worse original compositions.

How, especially in 1876, did Twain get away with it? Partly of course because he was a genius; but partly too because, as he declared in his preface, *Tom Sawyer* was "intended mainly for the entertainment of boys and girls,"[2] that is, not to be taken seriously. *Huckleberry Finn*, which was issued without this assurance, ran into trouble at once: it was called "vulgar" and "coarse" by critics and banned by the Concord Library in Massachusetts.

The greatest British juvenile author of the late nineteenth century, Lewis Carroll, was just as subversive as Twain, but in a more subtle way: it is appropriate that the original title of his first children's book should have been *Alice's Adventures Underground*. Modern critics have tended to see Carroll's heroine as exploring the inner world of the unconscious; but it is also possible to read *Alice's Adventures in Wonderland* and *Through the Looking-Glass* as underground literature in the social and political sense. The Walrus and the Carpenter have been described as caricatures of the rival politicians Benjamin Disraeli and William Gladstone, united in deceiving and devouring the innocent oysters, or voters, but in different styles. (This — at first sight farfetched — interpretation is given weight by Sir John Tenniel's illustrations, in which the Walrus sports Disraeli's elegant dress and luxuriant mustache, while the Carpenter has the square jaw and untidy clothes of Gladstone.)

The courts of the Queen of Hearts and the Red Queen, with their pompous formality and arbitrary laws of etiquette, can easily be seen as a grotesque version of the very proper and formal court of Queen Victoria, who also surrounded herself with extensive rose gardens and bowing courtiers. The King of Hearts, like Prince Albert, takes second place to his consort, while the Red King and the White King, though essential to the chess game upon which *Through the Looking-Glass* is based, hardly appear at all.

Carroll, unlike most of his contemporaries, was by no means awed by Queen Victoria. After *Alice's Adventures in Wonderland* had made him famous, the queen graciously signified through an intermediary that he might dedicate his next book to her. Carroll followed the letter rather than the spirit of this request, which was equivalent to a royal command: his next book, *Some Considerations on Determinants*, by Charles Dodgson, tutor in Mathematics of Christ Church, Oxford, was duly inscribed to Queen Victoria. *Through the Looking-Glass,* as it should have been, was dedicated to Alice Liddell, to whom the story had originally been told.

As one might expect from an Oxford don, the most thoroughgoing satirical attacks in the Alice books are directed at education. All the adults, especially those who resemble governesses or professors, are foolish, arbitrary, cruel, or mad. The only wholly decent and sensible person is Alice herself.

The Caterpillar, like a Victorian schoolmaster, asks unanswerable questions and demands that Alice repeat nonsense verses. Humpty-Dumpty, in the manner of some professors, asserts that he "can explain all the poems that ever were invented — and a good many that haven't been invented just yet."[3] He also manipulates statements to suit himself ("When *I* use a word . . . it means just what I choose it to mean"[4]). The Red Queen, like a mad governess, puts

Alice through a nightmare oral exam ("What's one and one and one and one and one and one and one and one and one and one and one?"[5]). The books are full of parodies of the moral verses found in contemporary school readers and of the rote question-and-answer method of teaching. The "regular course" of instruction followed by the Mock Turtle includes Ambition, Distraction, Uglification, and Derision, while the Gryphon goes to "the Classical master" to study Laughing and Grief: all the subjects that a child in the nineteenth century — or today — must learn in order to grow up and enter the adult world that Carroll hated.

Most radical of all at the time, though difficult to appreciate now, is the unconventional character of Alice herself. Except for her proper manners, she is by no means a good little girl in mid-Victorian terms. She is not gentle, timid, and docile, but active, brave, and impatient; she is highly critical of her surroundings and of the adults she meets. At the end of both books she fights back, reducing the Queen of Hearts' court to a pack of playing cards and the Red Queen to a kitten, crying "Who cares for *you?*"[6] and "I can't stand this any longer!"[7]

Both Twain and Carroll were split personalities in the social if not the technical sense of the term. As Samuel Clemens, Twain was a sentimental bourgeois paterfamilias, a would-be industrial magnate (he financed the manufacture of a typesetting machine that lost fifty thousand dollars) and a pillar of the community. Under the name Mark Twain he was a restless adventurer and a bitterly sardonic critic of the proper world his other self inhabited. "All the details of 'civilization' are legitimate matters for jeering," he wrote. "It is made up of about three tenths of reality and sincerity, and seven tenths of wind and humbug."[8] Charles Dodgson the Oxford don was prim, devout, obsessive, and painfully shy; occasionally he even refused to accept mail addressed to

Lewis Carroll, the affectionate and witty friend of little girls.

Other classic nineteenth-century authors, like Lewis Carroll's friend George MacDonald, were more consistently iconoclastic. MacDonald, who had been trained as a Congregational minister, became a follower of Novalis and Emanuel Swedenborg. He lost his pulpit because of his heretical ideas: he believed, contrary to current doctrine, that God's mercy was infinite and that not even the heathen would be damned forever. Though he was brought up in a deeply patriarchal society and faith, his most famous fairy tales, including *At the Back of the North Wind* and *The Princess and the Goblin,* describe a world in which supernatural power and goodness are centered in a mother-goddess figure who is both Life and Death; his child heroes and heroines must learn not only virtue but courage and independence.

Many other authors of juvenile classics, though not so openly unconventional as MacDonald or as strikingly divided in personality as Twain and Carroll, have had the ability to look at the world from below and note its less respectable aspects, just as little children playing on the floor can see the chewing gum stuck to the underside of polished mahogany tables and the hems of silk dresses held up with safety pins. The instinctive sympathy of such writers is often with the rebel, the defier of social laws.

Toad in Kenneth Grahame's *The Wind in the Willows,* for instance, is foolish, rash, and boastful as well as incorrigibly criminal — a kind of Edwardian upper-class juvenile delinquent, with a passion for flashy clothes and fast cars. Yet at the end of the book, only slightly chastened, Toad is restored to his ancestral home and given a triumphal banquet by his loyal friends. Grahame, who was a secretary of the Bank of England, lived a quiet and respectable life, but it is hard not to suspect that in imagination he was at least partly on the side of "Toad, the motor-car snatcher, the prison-breaker, the Toad who always escapes!"[9]

As we shall see later, opinions and attitudes that are not currently in style in the adult world often find expression in children's books of the time: theosophy and the new psychology in the work of Frances Hodgson Burnett, and Fabian socialism in that of E. Nesbit. During World War II, when "pacifist" was a dirty word, one of the most popular picture books for American children was Munro Leaf's *The Story of Ferdinand*. It is the tale of a gentle, noncombative — though very large and strong — bull who lives in Spain. All the other bulls "would fight each other all day. . . . butt each other and stick each other with their horns. . . . But not Ferdinand."[10] What he wants is to sit quietly under a tree and smell flowers. Taken to the bullring in Madrid, Ferdinand steadfastly refuses to fight and finally has to be sent home again, where he lives happily ever after. (According to experts, this cheerful ending would be unlikely in reality; insufficiently aggressive bulls are usually killed in the ring. And, of course, conscientious objectors in World War II often went to jail — but one can dream.)

In some famous children's books, the subversive message operates in the private rather than the public sphere. More or less openly, the author takes the side of the child against his or her parents, who are portrayed as at best silly and needlessly anxious, at worst selfish and stupid. In James Barrie's *Peter Pan*, discussed later, Mrs. Darling is charming but light-headed, while Mr. Darling is a bully and a hypocrite. In *Winnie-the-Pooh*, as we shall see, the adults who surround Christopher Robin are reduced to the status of stuffed toys.

Mr. and Mrs. Banks, the parents in P. L. Travers's *Mary Poppins*, are helpless and incompetent at managing their own household without the help of their magical nanny. At the start of *Mary Poppins Comes Back*, things have gotten so bad that they are on the verge of separation: " 'I don't know what's come over this house,' Mr. Banks went on. 'Nothing ever goes right — hasn't for ages! . . . I am going!' he said. 'And I don't know that I shall ever come back.' "[11]

Mrs. Banks, exhausted, sits on the stairs weeping while the servants (the Bankses are only middle-class, but this is 1935) drop trays of china and set the kitchen chimney on fire and the children scream and squabble in the nursery. When their mother's misery and helplessness are called to their attention, their reaction is cool and detached:

> "Children! Children!" Mrs. Banks was wringing her hands in despair. "Be quiet or I shall Go Mad!"
>
> There was silence for a moment as they stared at her with interest. Would she really? They wondered. And what would she be like if she did?[12]

Throughout the four volumes, it is clear that the children's real loyalty is to Mary Poppins.

Of course, not all famous children's literature is wholly subversive. Rudyard Kipling's Jungle Books, for example, appear to support the rule of law and order, but it is the law and order of the jungle, closer to that of colonial India than that of contemporary Britain. Each wild beast knows its place, and the duty of Mowgli the Wolf-Cub is to learn from his elders wisdom, courage, and the skills of survival. Against the exciting and glamorous jungle is set the petty existence of Mowgli's native village, with its gossip and suspicion and mob panic. Civilization — or, by inference, English middle-class life — is obviously less admirable and less character-forming than empire building. Like the rule of the British in India, of which Kipling was a strong supporter, the Jungle Books created an exciting, exotic world in which properly educated men could exercise authority over the "lesser breeds without the Law."[13] It is not by chance that Mowgli ends up as a game warden under British authority.

L. F. Baum's *The Wonderful Wizard of Oz* also contains no sweeping criticism of the status quo, even though Baum, as a failed South Dakota newspaper editor, must have been well acquainted with the hard times, low farm prices, and rise in freight rates that had ground down prairie families like Dorothy's. Instead, geography and climate are blamed for the fact that Aunt Em, once a "young, pretty wife," is "thin and gaunt, and never smiled, now" while Uncle Henry "worked hard from morning till night and did not know what joy was."[14]

The Wizard of Oz himself, however, combines the appearance of a Gilded Age politician with that of a medicine-show huckster, and in the central episode Dorothy and her friends expose him as a humbug whose powers and promises are as full of hot air as the balloon that eventually carries him back to Omaha. Baum is partially sympathetic to his hero, who as he says himself is "really a very good man" though "a very bad Wizard."[15] He allows the Wizard to give the Scarecrow a brain, the Cowardly Lion courage, and the Tin Woodman a heart — or rather, by a sort of benevolent hocus-pocus, to convince them that they are receiving what they already obviously have. The implication is that there is a place in American society for the self-improvement merchant, even if his magic is mere deception. It was an iconoclastic message at the time, but one that has since been upheld by hundreds of American politicians and by entrepreneurs of Wisdom, Confidence, and Self-Realization from Dale Carnegie to Shirley MacLaine.*

---

*An interesting reinterpretation of *The Wizard of Oz* emerged when the book was made into a film. To my own mind, the lush, semitropical vegetation and whimsical architecture of Oz have always suggested Southern California, where Baum spent his final years. In the 1939 MGM version, starring Judy Garland, the technicolor Land of Oz is the dream vision of a

Like Kipling, however, L. F. Baum did not approve of everything about his country. The social historian Henry M. Littlefield[16] has pointed out that Baum divided Oz into four kingdoms, of which two, the Gillikin Country in the north and the Quadling Country in the south, are ruled by good witches when Dorothy arrives — perhaps reflecting Baum's conscious or unconscious belief that Middle America was in fairly good shape. The Munchkins in the east, on the other hand, are ruled by a Wicked Witch, and she has transformed the originally human Woodman into a mechanical man who feels as if he has no heart — possibly a comment on the increasing industrialization and dehumanization of the eastern United States. As for the largely unsettled Winkie Country in the west, it is also dominated by a Wicked Witch, who threatens Dorothy and her friends with natural rather than mechanical dangers. Her attacking forces of wolves, crows, and bees may represent the danger to early settlers and farmers from wild animals, birds, and crop-destroying insects; and her

---

Depression farm girl, full of huge artificial-looking flowers and instant stucco castles. The center of this land is Los Angeles, and specifically Hollywood. To get there, you "follow the yellow brick road," which is not yellow in the film but golden — quite naturally, because it is made of money. The road leads to a walled city with considerable resemblance to the old MGM studios. Within, Dorothy finds a movie magnate's throne room and sound stage, where Oz manufactures his electronic illusions.

Oz, like Louis B. Mayer, has no real magic powers, so he cannot grant the wishes of Dorothy and her three companions — who in the film are also from Kansas and are Uncle Henry's farmhands. Oz cannot really give the Scarecrow a brain and the Tin Woodman a heart or make the Cowardly Lion brave, since these qualities — intelligence, love, and courage — are not available in Hollywood. But he can pretend to do so, which is all that is necessary. As representative Middle Americans, Dorothy's friends already have the qualities they are seeking. What they lack is faith in themselves, and Oz (metaphorically, MGM) can give them that — so his magic is real after all. Thus the film *The Wizard of Oz* is simultaneously an exposure, a defense, and a successful example of the role of Hollywood in American life at the time it was made.

Winged Monkeys, according to Mr. Littlefield, are Plains Indians.

TIME AND social change mute the revolutionary message of some children's classics. After more than a hundred years, Jo March of *Little Women* no longer seems so radical a tomboy: her untidiness, literary ambition, enthusiasm for "romps," and mild boyish slang ("Christopher Columbus!") appear tame. Her later career as a writer of Gothic thrillers and the director, with her husband, of a partially coeducational boarding school does not have the thrill it once did. Girls who love Louisa May Alcott's books today tend to be rather more quiet, feminine, and domestic than the average. But for at least five generations of American girls, Jo was a rebel and an ideal, and Louisa May Alcott's understanding of their own impatience with contemporary models of female behavior ("I hate affected, niminy-piminy chits!"[17] as Jo puts it) nothing less than miraculous.

In the second half of this century, as feminism launched its second wave, the limits of socially acceptable behavior for girls were steadily pushed back, and one "subversive" book after another was at first condemned and then applauded. When it first appeared, in 1964, Louise Fitzhugh's *Harriet the Spy* was criticized because its heroine secretly observed and dispassionately recorded the foolish behavior of adults. Its sequel, *The Long Secret* (1965), was censured because, for the first time in juvenile literature, it mentioned menstruation. Now both books are widely recommended. Astrid Lindgren's *Pippi Longstocking* was widely criticized when it was published in Sweden, in 1945. Today Pippi, who is careless of her appearance, mocks the school system, and can lick the circus strong man in a wrestling match, is an international favorite.

*

IT IS the particular gift of some writers to remain in a sense
children all their lives: to continue to see the world as boys
and girls see it and to take their side instinctively. One author
who carries on this tradition in contemporary America is Dr.
Seuss, who like Twain and Carroll has adopted a separate
literary personality (under his real name, Theodor Geisel, he
has been an editorial cartoonist, advertising artist, and
screenwriter). Seuss's picture books, though extremely popular with children, have yet to be recognized as classics; they
are not even mentioned in many surveys of the "best" children's books. Seuss is in good company here: *The Wonderful
Wizard of Oz* was similarly neglected for more than fifty years,
and Maurice Sendak's brilliant *Where the Wild Things Are —*
which suggests that children sometimes have violent, aggressive impulses toward their parents — was at first condemned as "too frightening" (frightening for whom? one wants
to ask).

From *And to Think That I Saw It on Mulberry Street*
(1937) onward, Dr. Seuss has not only celebrated the power
and richness of the child's imagination but suggested that
children may do well to conceal their flights of fancy from
their elders. The boy and girl in his best-known book, *The
Cat in the Hat,* shut indoors on a rainy day, completely wreck
the house with the help of the devilish-looking Cat, then tidy
it up again just before their mother gets home to ask:

"Did you have any fun?
Tell me. What did you do?"

And Sally and I
Did not know what to say.
Should we tell her the things
That went on there that day?

Should we tell her about it?
Now, what should we do?

Well . . .
What would YOU do
If your mother asked you?[18]

The implication is that Mother will never find out what went on in her absence — and just as well, too.

Grown-ups reading this story aloud may feel uneasy; we prefer to think of children as ingenuous and confiding. Usually, too, we like to believe that everything is all right in our immediate world and that the opinions and attitudes expressed in the popular media represent the full range of possible opinions and attitudes. But if by chance we should want to know what has been censored from establishment culture in the past, or what our kids are really up to today, we might do well to look at the classic children's books and listen to the rhymes being sung on school playgrounds.

2

Folktale Liberation

Folktales are the oldest and most widely known form of literature for children. "Beauty and the Beast" was told in classical Greece and ancient India; "Hansel and Gretel" has been collected in the West Indies, in African villages, and among the American Indians.

These tales also have another distinction: they are among the most subversive texts in children's literature. Often, though usually in disguised form, they support the rights of disadvantaged members of the population — children, women, and the poor — against the establishment. Law and order are not always respected: the master thief fools the count and the parson, and Jack kills the giant and steals his treasure. Rich people are often unlucky, afflicted, or helpless: kings and queens cannot have children or suffer from strange illnesses, while the poor are healthy and enterprising and fortunate.

As long as these stories remained part of an oral culture, related to small audiences of unimportant people, they were largely overlooked by the literary and educational establishment. But as soon as they began to surface in printed texts there were outcries of horror and disapproval; cries that have continued to this day.

The late-eighteenth-century author and educational authority Sarah Trimmer cautioned parents against allowing their children to hear or read fairy tales, which she considered immoral because they taught ambition, violence, a love of wealth, and the desire to marry above one's station. Cinderella, she wrote, "paints some of the worst passions that can enter into the human breast, and of which little children should, if possible, be totally ignorant; such as envy, jealousy, a dislike of step-mothers and half-sisters, vanity, a love of dress, etc."[1] Other critics complained that these tales were unscientific and confused truth with fiction, and that they wasted time that would be better spent learning facts, skills, and good manners.

More than 150 years later it was still believed in high-minded progressive circles that fairy tales were unsuitable for children. "Does not 'Cinderella' interject a social and economic situation which is both confusing and vicious? . . . Does not 'Jack and the Beanstalk' delay a child's rationalizing of the world and leave him longer than is desirable without the beginnings of scientific standards?"[2] as one child education expert, Lucy Sprague Mitchell, put it in the introduction to her *Here and Now Story Book*, which I received for my fifth birthday. It would be much better, she and her colleagues thought, for children to read simple, pleasant, realistic tales that would help to prepare us for the adult world.

Mrs. Mitchell's own contribution to literature was a squat volume, sunny orange in color, with an idealized city scene on the cover. Inside I could read about the Grocery Man ("This is John's Mother. Good morning, Mr. Grocery Man")[3] and How Spot Found a Home. The children and parents in these stories were exactly like the ones I knew, only more boring. They never did anything really wrong, and nothing dangerous or surprising ever happened to them — no more than it did to Dick and Jane, whom I and my friends were soon to meet in first grade.

After we grew up, of course, we found out how unrealistic these stories had been. The simple, pleasant adult society they had prepared us for did not exist. As we had suspected, the fairy tales had been right all along — the world was full of hostile, stupid giants and perilous castles and people who abandoned their children in the nearest forest. To succeed in this world you needed some special skill or patronage, plus remarkable luck; and it didn't hurt to be very good-looking. The other qualities that counted were wit, boldness, stubborn persistence, and an eye for the main chance. Kindness to those in trouble was also advisable — you never knew who might be useful to you later on.

The fairy tales were also way ahead of Mrs. Mitchell with respect to women's liberation. In her stories men drove wagons and engines and boats, built skyscrapers, worked in stores, and ran factories; women did nothing except keep house, look after children, and go shopping. Fairy tales, on the other hand, portrayed a society in which women were as competent and active as men, at every age and in every class. Gretel, not Hansel, defeated the witch; and for every clever youngest son there was a youngest daughter equally resourceful. The contrast continued in maturity, when women were often more powerful than men. Real help for the hero or heroine came most often from a fairy godmother or wise woman, and real trouble from a witch or wicked stepmother. With a frequency that recalls current feminist polemics, the significant older male figures were either dumb macho giants or malevolent little dwarfs.

Yet in spite of this, some contemporary feminists have joined the chorus of critics and attacked fairy tales as a male chauvinist form of literature: they believe that giving children stories like "Cinderella" and "Snow White" is a sort of brainwashing, intended to convince them that all little girls must be gentle, obedient, passive, and domestic while they wait patiently for their princes to come.

In a way these objections are understandable, since some of the tales we know best — those that have been popularized by Walt Disney, for instance — do have this kind of heroine. But from the point of view of European (and world) folklore, such stories are highly unrepresentative. The traditional tale, in fact, is exactly the sort of subversive literature of which a feminist should approve.

For one thing, these stories are in a literal sense women's literature. Charles Perrault, who was one of the first to write them down, called them "old wives' tales, governesses' and grannies' tales." Later, throughout Europe (except in Ireland), the storytellers from whom the Grimm brothers and their followers collected their material were most often women; in some areas, they were all women. For hundreds of years, while written literature was almost exclusively in the hands of men, these tales were being invented and passed on orally by women.

In content too fairy tales are women's literature. Writers like Robert Graves have seen them as survivals of an older, matriarchal culture and faith; but whether they are right or not, it is women who most often are the central characters in many of these stories, and women who have the supernatural power. In the Grimms' original *Children's and Household Tales* (1812), there are sixty-one women and girl characters who have magic powers as against only twenty-one men and boys: and these men are usually dwarfs and not humans.

Another thing that separates the folktale from the printed literature of its time is that it is a middle- and working-class genre. The world it portrays and the problems it deals with are those of farmers, artisans, shopkeepers, and the working poor: survival, employment, family unity. The heroes and heroines of these tales are often very badly off, while the supernatural villains — the giants and ogres and

witches — are rich. "Kings" and "queens," who lack supernatural powers and have human problems — infertility, exterior enemies, serious illness — seem from internal
evidence to be merely well-to-do farmers. Literary retellings
of the tales, however, from Perrault to the present, usually
give their royalty a convincingly aristocratic setting.

The handful of folktales that most readers today know
are not typical of the genre. They are the result of a more
insidious sort of critical attack than that mounted by Sarah
Trimmer and her heirs: the skewed selection and silent revision of subversive texts. At first this selection and revision
were open and acknowledged. Perrault rewrote the stories
he had heard from his "old wives" in elegant seventeenth-
century French, adding witty morals in verse and turning the
wise women of folk tradition into pretty fairies in court dress
with sparkling wands and butterfly wings. In midnineteenth-
century England, George Cruikshank made his four favorite
tales into temperance tracts — at Cinderella's wedding, he
reported, a great bonfire was made of all the bottles of wine
and spirits in the castle. Even the Grimm brothers openly
bowdlerized their stories to make them "suitable for childhood,"[4] and, as time went on, altered them in other ways.
In each subsequent edition of the tales, for instance, women
were given less to say and do.[5]

Most compilers of books of fairy tales, unfortunately,
have been less direct. For nearly two hundred years tales
have been omitted and unacknowledged changes made in the
original texts. The stories we know best today reflect the
taste of the literary men who edited the first popular collections of fairy stories for children during the nineteenth century. They read the hundreds of folktales that had been
gathered by scholars, chose the ones that most appealed to
them as conventional upper-middle-class Victorians, and then

rewrote these tales to make them suitable for Victorian children.

By the late nineteenth century a canon had been established, and the dozen or so tales these editors had liked best were reprinted again and again. "Sleeping Beauty" was retold over and over, always without its original ending, in which the heroine gives birth to two children as the result of the prince's passionate awakening of her. Meanwhile, "The Sleeping Prince," a parallel story about a passive hero rescued from enchantment by an active heroine, was forgotten.

Folktales recorded in the field are full of everything the Victorian editors left out: sex, death, low humor, and especially female initiative. In some more recent and comprehensive books of tales — as well as in Andrew Lang's famous fairy books named after colors, the later volumes of which were largely compiled and revised by his wife — there are more active heroines. They travel to the world's end, cross oceans on a wild goose's back, climb mountains of glass, enter giants' castles and steal magic objects, outwit false suitors, and defeat all kind of supernatural enemies. They work for years to release their lovers or relatives from enchantments and help them to escape from witches and ogres. They are in effect liberated women who have courage, intelligence, resourcefulness, endurance, and kind hearts.

EVEN IN edited versions, fairy tales — as hostile critics have recognized — can be dangerous; and today bookstores are still full of bowdlerized and skewed volumes in which the energy and excitement and vivid detail of the stories are missing or watered down. Sometimes this is done through the illustrations, which are either artificially cute in a comic book style or sentimentally vague, muting the strong impact of events and characters under romantic watercolor washes of pink and blue. Such pictures are unpopular with children, who do not believe that the imaginative is identical with the vague; they notice and object when the witch's house is obviously not made of gingerbread. Even more depressing and inappropriate are pictures that derive from modern art and run to heavily patterned woodcuts or silk-screen prints in muddy shades of green and purple, in which it is impossible to tell the princess from the wallpaper.

A more serious problem in many of these collections is the stories themselves. Some of them lazily reprint the Victorian versions of the tales; but even when an editor has conscientiously gone back to the original, there are difficulties. Is one to reproduce the version collected in the field, or should one retell the story with the object of making it more literary, easier for children to understand, or less disturbing?

Fidelity to the original might seem at first the best choice, but it is not as easy as that. The semiliterate, elderly rural people who are folklorists' usual informants tend to speak in dialect; they repeat themselves and sometimes forget episodes. Perhaps as a result, Perrault's "Little Red Riding-Hood" ends with both the heroine and her grandmother eaten alive. No last-minute arrival of the woodsman, no miraculous surgical operation, no punishment of the wolf. The Grimms collected two different endings to the story: in one version the wolf is drowned, while in the other his belly is filled with stones and he falls down dead.[6]

Even today sentimental editors still bowdlerize and rewrite, often without admitting it. They speed up the appearance of the woodsman so that he walks in just after the villain has growled his immortal last line, "The better to eat you with, my dear!" The wolf is chased out the door and disappears in the forest; Grandmother comes out of the closet, where she has been hiding, or returns home from the village.

Nobody gets eaten, nobody gets rescued, nobody gets punished. This is supposed to make children feel safer — even though the wolf is still wandering around outside somewhere, waiting for the next little girl. Which is possibly truer to current social conditions — but hardly more reassuring.

IN SPITE OF all the damage that has been done by well-meaning editors, fairy tales continue to fascinate and haunt us; and they have their defenders as well as their critics. The psychoanalyst Bruno Bettelheim, in *The Uses of Enchantment,* set out to rescue the tales from what he saw as a horde of hostile and disapproving colleagues, who considered them unrealistic, immoral, and violent. In his view, this prejudice can have serious and destructive social effects:

> I have known many examples where, particularly in late adolescence, years of belief in magic are called upon to compensate for the person's having been deprived of it prematurely in childhood. . . . Many young people who today suddenly seek escape in drug-induced dreams, apprentice themselves to some guru, believe in astrology, engage in practicing "black magic," or who in some other fashion escape from reality into daydreams about magic experiences which are to change their life for the better, were prematurely pressed to view reality in an adult way.[7]

Though some of Bettelheim's interpretations seem overdetermined by orthodox Freudianism, his approach is in the main thoughtful, humane, and sensitive. One of his most interesting insights is that the various protagonists of a story often represent conflicting motives or emotions within a single individual. The ambitious, single-minded brother who has no time to waste on an old beggar woman or a wounded animal and the good-natured simpleton who shares his last piece of bread are the same fellow in different moods: the tale shows the consequences of different choices. The fairy godmother and the witch are two versions of the same woman, and the wicked stepmother is our own mother seen by black light after the blissful years of babyhood are over.

Another psychologist who has defended folktales is the transactional analyst Eric Berne (the author of *Games People Play*), who points out that folks remember the tales that matter most to them. He claims that your favorite fairy story is as much a giveaway of character and life history as your most recurrent dream. The boy who once admired Jack the Giant Killer has grown up to work for Ralph Nader; the girl who loved the tale "The Frog Prince" is married now to an ugly but very successful man, while the one who preferred "Little Red Riding-Hood" still keeps getting deceived and seduced, often with rather nasty consequences for her seducer.

BUT IT IS not necessary to be a psychologist to understand folktales. Often, the hidden messages lie just under the surface. "Snow White," for instance, could be seen as telling girls to beware of a mother or stepmother who is secretly competitive and envious of their youth and good looks. The gifts and advice of such a mother are poisonous and designed not to make you more attractive but to immobilize you in a kind of death in life. In extreme cases it might be best to run away and live with friends. Even the horrifying ending, in which the wicked queen dances in red-hot shoes till she drops, suggests a real-life equivalent: the middle-aged woman who exhausts herself by insisting on upstaging her daughter and being the life of the party. "Red Riding-Hood," in this reading, not only warns against predatory men but against the sort of grandmother who wants to devour her grandchild emotionally and announces her intent by crying, "You're so cute I could just eat you up!"

"Jack the Giant Killer" can be seen as a lesson about how to deal with the big, stupid, mean, and ugly people you are going to meet in life, a more useful lesson than that taught by video games. Jack doesn't zap the giant with a laser gun, because in real life when you meet a bully or an armed mugger or a boss who wants to push you around you probably won't have a laser gun. What Jack does is to defeat the giant by using his intelligence and powers of invention.

As with individuals, so with societies. Each nation and generation chooses its favorite stories from the hundreds available and alters them to suit local beliefs and conditions. Cinderella appears as a ninth-century Chinese maiden, and her story is told today, anthropologists report, by the Arabs of North Africa and the Zuni Indians of New Mexico — where her fairy godmother is a wild turkey. In the Scottish Highlands, on the other hand, she is Cinderella's dead mother come back to life in the form of a wise old sheep.

Anthropologists of the structuralist school have noticed that almost every popular European fairy story begins with the description of a family situation. "Once upon a time there was a poor woodcutter who lived near the forest with his wife and two children . . ." or "Long ago there lived a king and queen who had a daughter as beautiful as the day . . ." The endings of these tales are often alike too: "So they were married, and lived happily ever after." The story itself is about the period of time between the hero's or heroine's leaving their family of origin and the establishment of a new family of procreation. Between these two events lie many adventures that are also tests — tests of virtue, courage, cleverness, patient endurance, or kindness of heart.

In another popular type of fairy story, such as "Hansel

and Gretel," the hero and heroine remain children throughout. They too go through adventures and tests; they are lost in the forest, threatened by cannibalistic witches and giants. But their happy ending comes when they are restored to their family of origin. One purpose of such tales, according to a colleague of mine, is to express and relieve the two basic but opposed fears of all children (and a good many grown-ups): that they will be abandoned, and that they will be devoured. Adults who prefer these tales to the first type may still be stuck in their own childhood.

The structuralists have noticed, too, that the hero or heroine of a fairy tale usually cannot kill the dragon or marry the princess without help. This, of course, is contrary to the American tradition that if you go it alone and work hard enough, you will get to the top. In fairy tales, characters who refuse help, or refuse to help others, end up covered with tar or talking frogs and snakes. If the compiler of a book of fairy stories doesn't see things this way, he can edit out such tales in favor of ones like "The Gallant Tailor" or "Mollie Whuppie," in which the protagonists make it completely on their own.

The great distinction of the Grimm brothers was that though they altered their tales, they did not pick and choose; they printed almost everything they heard. The complete edition of their *Household Tales* contains two hundred stories and runs to nearly 650 pages of small type in the standard American edition. Only about eighty of these tales involve magic — the rest are a mixed bag of jokes, fables, legends, comic anecdotes, and ghost stories. They were told not only to children but (as the name implies) to the whole family.

Though Christian saints appear in some of the stories, the Grimms' tales can also be seen as a kind of pagan Bible, garbled and altered by being passed down orally through many generations but still full of the half-animal gods and familiar spirits of pre-Christian Europe — the haunted wells and forests, the elves and witches, the ancient superstitions and rituals. As with the Bible, every reader or editor can take from it what suits him or her.

An excellent sampling of the unfamiliar *Household Tales* is contained in *The Juniper Tree and Other Tales from Grimm,* selected by Lore Segal and Maurice Sendak. They have included a few old favorites, but more are missing; and the stories that replace them are among the strangest, most grotesque, mysterious, and haunting in Grimm. Some are not fairy tales at all but half-comic, half-frightening realistic stories of violence, deception, and folly; and by no means all end happily.

Even the tales of magic, for a modern reader, have odd symbolic overtones. In "Hans My Hedgehog," for instance, a peasant's wife gives birth to a child who is a hedgehog from the waist up; he rides on a cock and can play the bagpipes better than any man in the country. His parents do not care much for him and make him sleep on a pile of straw behind the stove: "So there he lay behind the oven for eight years and his father got tired of him and thought, If he would only die! He did not die, however, but went on lying there."[8]

In the tale "Godfather Death," Death takes his young godson into the woods and shows him an herb that grows there, saying,

> "I shall make you into a famous doctor. When you are called to a patient's bedside I will appear and if I stand at the sick man's head you can boldly say that you will cure him and if you give him some of this herb he will recover. But if I stand at the sick man's feet, then he is mine, and you must say there is no help for him and no doctor on this earth could save him."[9]

The godson becomes rich and successful; but finally he oversteps himself and angers Death — like some modern physicians — by keeping a patient alive when he knows she should die. He pays with his own life.

The same fantastic and haunting quality appears in the illustrations to *The Juniper Tree*. Like all Maurice Sendak's work, they are superb. But they come from a darker and stranger side of his genius than the pictures in *In the Night Kitchen* or *Where the Wild Things Are*. They are visions of another and in some ways realer world than this, a dream — or nightmare — world certainly, but one in which the dream gardens contain actual toads, complete to the last wart. They have beauty too, though it is a beauty that sometimes merges into the terrifying: skeletons appear, corpses, hooded ghosts, and a devil that makes the Wild Things look like stuffed toys.

The late J.R.R. Tolkien once wrote, "If fairy story as a kind is worth reading at all it is worthy to be written for and read by adults. They will, of course, put more in and get more out than children can."[10] *The Juniper Tree* is for adults, who can read these strange old tales as if they had been written yesterday by Jorge Luis Borges, Italo Calvino, or I. B. Singer and who will, if they are fortunate, find them a way into a lost world, not only of childhood, but of universal power and meaning.

3

Fairy Tale Fiction

FITZGERALD TO UPDIKE

There is an underground connection between fairy tales and modern fiction — between one of the oldest forms of literature and one of the most recent. More often than we realize, the stock situations and stock characters, especially the female characters, of the classic fairy tale reappear in the novels we read today. They don't appear only in novels, of course: they turn up in films, plays, poetry, comic strips, advertisements, and dreams — and also in real life, which as usual imitates art.

In the best-known folktales there are several possible roles for the adult male protagonist. He may be a prince, a poor but ambitious boy, a fortunate fool, a traveling vagabond, or a clever trickster. But if you are the female protagonist of one of the fairy tales most popular today, there are only two possibilities: either you are a princess or you are an underprivileged but basically worthy girl who is going to become a princess if she is brave and good and lucky.

If you are already a princess when the story starts, you usually have a problem. Very likely you need rescuing from some danger or enchantment. Maybe you have been promised to a dragon or promised yourself to a dragon; or you might have been kidnapped by a witch or enchanter, who asks impossible riddles or sets impossible tasks for your would-be rescuers. Possibly it is your father, the king, who has set these tasks. Or perhaps you are just very difficult to please, like the princess in "King Thrushbeard," and set the tasks or riddles yourself, to drive away possible suitors.

The disadvantage — or, if you prefer it, the advantage — of being a princess is that you are essentially passive. You just sit there on your throne, or on a nearby rock, while the suitors and the dragons fight it out. In an extreme form of this passivity you are literally asleep or in a trance like Sleeping Beauty or Snow White. This particular archetype is one that has always appealed to men, and it turns up again and again in their fiction. The trance takes different forms: sometimes it is physical virginity, sometimes it is a sort of psychic virginity. Often the princess is frigid, or sexually unawakened like Lady Chatterley; sometimes she is intellectually or politically unawakened, like Gwendolen Harleth in *Daniel Deronda* or like the Princess Casamassima in Henry James's novel of the same name, which is in many ways, and not always successfully, very much like a fairy tale.

One especially interesting version of the Sleeping Beauty story occurs in F. Scott Fitzgerald's *Tender Is the Night.* Fitzgerald, of course, was deeply attracted to the princess type of girl, and most of his heroines are American princesses — very beautiful, very popular, and usually very rich. He realized this quite well himself and often used fairy tale material deliberately, as in "The Diamond as Big as the Ritz," in which the hero discovers a twentieth-century version of the enchanted castle in the mountains of Nevada.

Fitzgerald's early stories, like his early life, were almost literally fairy tales. The handsome prince — or if not quite a prince, at least a baronet — always won the beautiful princess, just as Fitzgerald had won Zelda Sayre, the most beau-

tiful and popular girl in Montgomery, or possibly even
Alabama. As time passed and things began to go wrong his
stories changed. *The Beautiful and Damned* begins where
most fairy tales end, with the marriage of the handsome,
charming prince and the beautiful, gay princess. But instead
of living happily ever after, they begin to waste their youth
and wealth: they give endless drunken parties and quarrel
meaninglessly. Anthony's uncle hears of this behavior and
disinherits him, and Anthony spends the rest of his time and
money in an attempt to break the will. In the end he succeeds,
and he and Gloria inherit the kingdom; but it is too late. They
are still just as good as they are beautiful, but by now that
is not so very beautiful.

Nicole Warren, the golden-haired heroine of *Tender Is
the Night,* is also an American princess, the daughter of what
Fitzgerald describes as one of the "great feudal families" of
the Middle West, and fabulously rich. But she is under a
really bad spell — she is mad and confined to a clinic in Switz-
erland, a sort of enchanted castle presided over by Swiss
psychiatrist dwarfs. Even the cause of her madness has a
folktale parallel, in the story known as "Cap O'Rushes," one
version of which was the source of *King Lear*. In this tale a
widowed king falls violently in love with his own golden-haired
daughter and declares that he intends to marry her. She hears
of the plan and runs away into the forest disguised in a cloak
made of a hundred different kinds of animal fur and skin —
a sort of external split personality. Nicole Warren is not so
lucky: her father seduces her before she can escape, and she
becomes schizophrenic.

Fitzgerald's hero, Dick Diver, is a poor clergyman's son
from Buffalo who has already won several magic prizes, including a Rhodes scholarship from Yale and an M.D. from
Johns Hopkins. He has also had the best supernatural help:
psychiatric training with Freud in Vienna. He goes to the

sanitarium, breaks the enchantment, rescues Nicole, and marries her.

But the story does not end there. Dick begins to fall under a bad spell himself, the spell of Nicole's wealth. He gives up his job at the clinic and moves with her to a grand house on the Riviera. He is supposed to be writing a great book, but he spends less and less time on it. Instead the Divers become what are now known as Beautiful People. They give fabulous parties, and Dick falls in love with a young movie actress. As his former partner's wife says, he is no longer a serious person. Another hero carries Nicole off, and Dick Diver is banished to a provincial town in upstate New York — in Fitzgerald's view a fate worse than death.

Tender Is the Night is also extremely interesting from a women's liberation point of view. Nicole is not permanently cured by marrying Dick, but only when she stops being dependent on him and stands alone. She is able to achieve independence for rather old-fashioned reasons — with the help of another man and because she is so rich. The other heroine of the novel, Rosemary Hoyt, is independent in a more modern way: she is a successful actress. When Rosemary falls in love with Dick, her mother encourages her to go as far as she likes, saying shrewdly: "Whatever happens it can't spoil you because economically you're a boy, not a girl."[1] In other words, Rosemary doesn't have to keep herself chaste so that she will be worth more to some man. She can support herself and have whatever experiences she likes.

In contrast to the financially independent woman is the economically dependent man. As Dick Diver gives up his profession and ceases to be a "serious person," his value comes to depend more and more on so-called female accomplishments: his good looks, his skill as a host, his entertaining conversation, his ability to charm, and even his sexual fidelity.

Like the nineteenth-century Victorian lady, once he loses these qualities he is finished.

In fiction, Fitzgerald seems to have recognized that men and women both are at their best when they are independent and have some serious work. But he could not put these principles into practice; he could not allow Zelda to become independent of him or to have her own career. She had to remain an idle princess, and her tale ended where Nicole's began: in a mental asylum.

THE STORY of the poor girl who overcomes obstacles and makes a good marriage in the end, what might be called the Horatia Alger story, is very common in nineteenth-century fiction, especially fiction written by women. This heroine does not have to begin in absolute poverty — even Cinderella's family must have been middle-class or her stepsisters wouldn't have been able to go to the ball in such style. But she does have to be in some way underprivileged at the start of the book, and she must go through many difficulties before she can marry the prince.

Occasionally she is poor in other than the economic sense, as with some of Jane Austen's heroines: Catherine Morland of *Northanger Abbey* is poor in intellect; Marianne Dashwood of *Sense and Sensibility* is naive and muddleheaded; while Fanny Price of *Mansfield Park* is (as Lionel Trilling has pointed out) poor in spirit. Charlotte Brontë, even more daring, made the heroine of *Villette* plain.

The most classic nineteenth-century Cinderella story is probably *Jane Eyre*. The beginning of the book especially conforms to the pattern: Jane's aunt, Mrs. Reed, and her three cousins are as awful as any stepmother and stepsisters. The theme is repeated when Jane goes away to school and is persecuted by teachers and students alike. The fairy godmother who helps her is also a teacher, Miss Temple, and her further adventures have other fairy tale parallels.

When I began to look for a modern Cinderella, I had more difficulty. The story is still being written, but not for an intellectual audience. The women's magazines and the contemporary gothic novel are full of it, and (if we are to judge from the newspapers) it occurs frequently in real life. But serious women writers apparently no longer believe in upwardly mobile marriage as a happy ending. Even Edith Wharton, seventy or eighty years ago, didn't believe in it: *The House of Mirth* is a devastating account of a Cinderella who doesn't catch the prince and finally can't even marry a toad; and in *The Custom of the Country* the prince goes off with the ugly sister.

For a Cinderella story by a first-rate modern writer I had to go back to Jean Stafford's *Boston Adventure,* published in 1944. This book — which was a tremendous popular and critical success for a first novel — is also interesting because it contains an impressive fairy godmother character who turns out to be a kind of witch.

Sonia Marburg, the heroine of *Boston Adventure,* is the daughter of a poor cobbler who lives in a seaside resort north of Boston. Her parents are so hard up that they can't afford to buy a bed for her, so she sleeps on the floor. When Sonia is twelve her father deserts the family, and she goes to work as a housemaid for three dollars a week to support her mother and her horrible baby brother, who is a sort of vicious fairy changeling. For years the person in the world Sonia has most admired has been a formidable aristocratic spinster lady named Miss Pride who comes to the hotel where Sonia works every summer. Her persistent fantasy is that Miss Pride will adopt her and take her to live on Beacon Hill.

One proof that *Boston Adventure* is a fairy tale is that Sonia gets her wish. Her awful little brother dies, and her mother goes mad; Sonia is about to quit school and take a job as cook to a vulgar and ill-natured dentist's family (complete with mean, overdressed stepsister) when she is rescued. Miss Pride appears in her magic Rolls-Royce and whisks her away to a house in Louisburg Square. There Miss Pride educates her, buys her new clothes, teaches her manners, and introduces her to Boston society — in its own way, a world as strange as the enchanted kingdoms of fairy tales. But Sonia never gets to marry the prince. For one thing, the only really eligible prince marries a pedigreed Boston princess. Besides, Miss Pride does not want to let Sonia go — she is determined to keep her as a companion until she dies. So she scolds her, bribes her, threatens her, and warns her that with "insanity in the family" she would be wicked to marry. And Miss Pride wins.

IN THE TRADITIONAL folktale, as in *Boston Adventure,* the fairy godmother and the witch are not always separate characters but sometimes merge into each other. At one end of the spectrum is the totally wicked, cannibalistic witch of "Hansel and Gretel." Somewhat less destructive is the witch who, like Miss Pride, keeps a girl in luxurious captivity; the best-known version of this tale is probably "Rapunzel," in which the witch shuts her adopted daughter up in a tower that she enters by using the girl's long hair as a ladder. Then there are characters like Mother Holle who do not want to possess the heroine forever but demand her company and services for a long time, usually seven years. At the end of this period the girl is rewarded and sent home. Finally there are fairy godmothers like Cinderella's who reward you without asking anything in return.

The other fairy tale character related to the witch is the stepmother. These categories often overlap: a lot of stepmothers are witches, and some witches are stepmothers —

or even mothers. The wicked stepmother-witch we know best, the one in "Snow White," was a mother in the original story the brothers Grimm collected. They changed it in the printed version, thinking her behavior unnatural.

English and American fiction is full of wicked stepmother figures, from Miss Murdstone of *David Copperfield* on. In more recent novels the disguise is often thrown aside, and the real mother is revealed as a witch who has deliberately cast a spell over her child, though her methods are those described by Freud rather than Frazer.

A beautiful example of this witch in a current novel is Sophie Portnoy, in Philip Roth's *Portnoy's Complaint:*

> She was so deeply imbedded in my consciousness that for the first year of school I seem to have believed that each of my teachers was my mother in disguise. As soon as the last bell had sounded, I would rush off for home, wondering as I ran if I could possibly make it to our apartment before she had succeeded in transforming herself. Invariably she was already in the kitchen by the time I arrived, and setting out my milk and cookies. Instead of causing me to give up my delusions, however, the feat merely intensified my respect for her powers. And then it was always a relief not to have caught her between incarnations anyway — even if I never stopped trying. I knew that my father and sister were innocent of my mother's real nature, and the burden of betrayal that I imagined would fall to me if I ever came upon her unawares was more than I wanted to bear at the age of five. I think I even feared that I might have to be done away with were I to catch sight of her flying in from school through the bedroom window, or making herself emerge, limb by limb, out of an invisible state and into her apron.[2]

Sophie Portnoy can fly, make herself invisible, and transform herself into other shapes — and that's not all, as we find out later. Her husband has no magic powers; he is barely getting by as an insurance agent and suffers from severe constipation. (It isn't suggested that his affliction is caused by his wife, but since on her own admission she can "accomplish anything,"[3] it seems likely that she could cure him — if she wanted to.)

As soon as Alex is old enough he escapes from the witch, though not without considerable difficulty. He goes out into the world like any fairy tale hero and conquers various semihuman female antagonists, including one called the Pumpkin and another named Monkey. But he has not broken the witch's spell, and she gets him in the end when he rashly goes to Israel, his mother country. Transforming herself into an Israeli girl, but still recognizable by her red hair and freckles, she defeats Alex after a long struggle in which he is physically victorious but sexually demolished. This sends him straight to the couch of a psychiatrist, Dr. Spielvogel (Play-Bird) — the magical animal helper of the folktale who has appeared in the story unusually, but perhaps not fatally, late.

The wise women of modern fiction come from all classes of society. Some, like Virginia Woolf's Mrs. Ramsay and E. M. Forster's Mrs. Wilcox, are upper-class or upper middle-class. Others, such as William Faulkner's Dilsey and the cook Berenice Brown in Carson McCullers's *The Member of the Wedding,* are servants. Many of them are also in a sense nature goddesses whose power is related to a semimagical connection with the earth, the seasons, and the processes of growth and creation. They can be recognized by their knowledge of plants, their instinctive sympathy with children and animals, and their intuition, which sometimes operates at the level of ESP. (One way we know that Miss Pride of *Boston Adventure* is a bad fairy godmother is that she dislikes plants and children and is cruel to her cat. But in another sense she too is an earth goddess: some of her power comes through money, but most is derived from her position in society. In a very Bostonian way, she draws her strength from the past: from the earth of the graveyards where her ancestors are buried, and which she is so fond of visiting.)

A PARTICULARLY interesting example of the wise woman in a contemporary novel is Mrs. Robinson in John Updike's brilliant short novel *Of the Farm*. This is the story, told in the first person by an advertising man named Joey Robinson, of his visit with his new second wife and stepson to the Pennsylvania farm where he grew up and where his widowed mother now lives alone. The main action of the book is the conflict between Mrs. Robinson and her new daughter-in-law, Peggy. Peggy is what has been called a man's woman. She is approvingly compared by her husband to a submissive "concubine in chains"[4] who "knew herself only in my love for her"[5] and is said to have a "mythology, of women giving themselves to men, of men in return giving women a reason to live."[6]

Peggy, though a natural beauty, is a "city wife," an *"habituée* of foyers and elevators"[7] not at all at home in the country. She goes blackberry picking in a bikini top and gets badly scratched — and half the berries she picks are green. Frightened by a passing car, she hides in what turns out to be a thicket of poison ivy.

Mrs. Robinson, on the other hand, does not need any man to give her a reason to live. She exists for herself and in relation to the farm, which has been in her family for generations. She knows the name of every plant, bird, and animal on the eighty acres and spares the birds' nests and the best wildflowers when she mows the fields. She declares impatiently to Peggy that she has never believed in the "psy-

chological differences" between men and women. Unlike
Peggy, she believes in God; but when she hears a sermon
in church about Eve's subservience to Adam, her only comment is "I get so tired of men talking about women."[8] But
she is also not interested in dominating or limiting men. She
tells Peggy's eleven-year-old son that he can drive her trac-
tor, but Peggy refuses to permit it, causing one of the worst
quarrels in the book.

Mrs. Robinson is compared by her son both to a goddess
and a witch. "With her hair down she had seemed witchlike
to me ever since as a child I would watch her brushing it in
the . . . yard so that birds might weave her shed hair into
their nests."[9] (She also refers to herself as an "old witch.")
When she tells a story to Peggy's son, the narrator says that
his "eyes had the shininess of the enchanted — the frogs and
deer who are princes."[10]

In spite of her powers Mrs. Robinson lacks serenity —
she is dying and knows it; she knows she will never see her
grandchildren again and that her son will sell the farm after
she dies because of Peggy's greed for profit. "She wants the
money sitting in these acres. . . . You've taken a vulgar
woman to be your wife,"[11] she says, and Joey admits it.

In a final quarrel, Peggy accuses Mrs. Robinson of being
in fact a witch: "Peggy's idea . . . was that my mother had
undervalued and destroyed my father, had been inadequately
a 'woman' to him, had brought him to a farm which was in
fact her giant lover."[12] The quarrel terrifies Joey: "Their conversation seemed a collision of darknesses to me but my
mother's darkness was nurturing whereas Peggy's was cold,
dense, and metallic. . . . Her cigarette smoke insulted the
room."[13]

The moral victory is Mrs. Robinson's, but the practical
triumph will probably be Peggy's. The farm will be sold, partly
because Peggy wants the money and partly because she

recognizes Joey's love for the place and cannot bear to share
him with it. The militantly unliberated woman like Peggy has
to possess her man totally, because she exists only in relation
to him. Like some of the witches in the folktales, she has no
true shape of her own; even if she does not bear her husband
any ill will, she must wrap herself around him and cling like
a vine, finally choking him. In the end, this new variety of
witch is worse than the old, and allows a man less freedom.

4

Braking for Elves

FASHIONABLE FOLKLORE

FOR ADULTS

In the 1970s and early 1980s, when many strange social phenomena occurred, there was a proliferation of fads and cults, some of Eastern or quasi-Eastern origin, others home-grown. One of the most widespread, though least recognized, was the fascination with fairies, elves, gnomes, unicorns, dragons, and the like, which continues to some extent today. Though it never became an organized faith, at its height it attracted more followers than est, Dianetics, Krishna Consciousness, or Sun Myung Moon and sold millions of books, posters, calendars, and T-shirts. Like other cults of the time it appealed mainly to young people, often the most privileged and best educated among them: in a survey of 350 undergraduates at Brown University, for instance, nearly 100 declared that they believed in hobbits, while only 40 claimed to believe in angels.

It could be said, of course, that the Brown students were kidding, making a fashionable joke; that none of them was anywhere near as deeply involved as believers in Dianetics or Zen Buddhism or the unfortunate followers of the Reverend Jim Jones. Though they might spray paint FRODO

LIVES on public buildings or paste bumper stickers reading
I BRAKE FOR ELVES on their VWs, they didn't "really believe" in such beings.

In a sense this is quite true. For most of its adherents
pixiolatry was not a separatist cult but a conventional, even
an establishment, religion in which the members mainly went
through the motions, experiencing in the process a shallow,
warm glow of good feeling rather than the deep, hot tremors
of true faith. The college student who owned the complete
authorized version of Tolkien together with the relevant study
guides and concordances, and attended regular meetings of
the Fantasy and Sci Fi Club, was no more (and no less)
committed than his or her politely agnostic parents, who kept
their Bible next to the *New York Times Cook Book* and attended church or temple only on holidays or for weddings
and funerals. In both cases, what mattered was not inner
conviction but outward observance, which identified the follower of Frodo or God socially and culturally.

This is not, of course, to claim that the content of a
belief system is unimportant. As John Updike says in *The
Coup,* "What matters in a myth, a belief, is . . . Does it
enable us to live, to keep going? . . . the crucial question
isn't Can you prove it? but Does it give us a handle on the
reality that otherwise would overwhelm us?"[1] What was interesting was that for so many young people, the God of their
parents was not enough.

I first became aware of the new faith of pixiolatry when
my attention was called to the startlingly large sales of books
that were guides not only to Tolkien but to minor supernatural
beings in general. What set these books apart from earlier
works on similar subjects was that they were presented —
sometimes, but not always, with a wink — as nonfiction; they
invited their readers to share the assumption that goblins and

sprites exist and can be identified on a country walk as if they were mockingbirds or mushrooms. Some of these books were obvious fast-food reprints, like *The World Guide to Gnomes, Fairies, Elves, and Other Little People* (1978), which was nothing but Thomas Keightley's classic *Fairy Mythology,* first published in 1850 (and thus conveniently out of copyright), warmed up in the publisher's microwave oven and served with a new title and a pretty Richard Doyle jacket.

A more serious effort along the same lines was *A Field Guide to the Little People* (1977), by Nancy Arrowsmith and George Moorse. Its authors went back to the original, often nineteenth-century sources (including Keightley) for their material, and they provided a good bibliography and index. A significant term here, as with the *World Guide,* was "Little People." In common discourse the Little People are not usually elves but, semifacetiously, children; or else they are what used to be called before feminism the Little Man or the Man in the Street. Supernatural power was thus half-consciously claimed for the most powerless among us — children and the anonymous, almost invisible ordinary citizen. Certainly, in a world that was growing increasingly violent, impersonal, and centralized, this was a reassuring faith. Pixiolatry also proposed that supernatural power was to be found not in great cities, but in out-of-the-way rural locations: in forgotten villages, isolated farmhouses, untidy patches of woods, lonely streams and hills: an agreeable fantasy for readers conscious of the concentration of other sorts of power in other places.

Arrowsmith and Moorse carry out the "nature guide" charade unevenly. On the one hand, they solemnly list an identification and a habitat for each imaginary creature, and nowhere in the book is there the least hint that hobgoblins and pixies and trolls are imaginary. But the arrangement is unscientific — neither geographical, alphabetical, nor by species — and the spooky, sketchy illustrations don't always match the text. Though the descriptions are entertaining, many of the illustrative folktales that are included are over-condensed and rather clumsily retold.

The *Field Guide,* unlike most contemporary works of pixiology, covers all of Europe, and its haphazard arrangement does point up some interesting differences between the spirits of different countries. In every nation, folk tradition seems to produce two classes of supernatural being. In one the national type is idealized; in the other it is mocked or caricatured. So in Ireland we have the heroic fairies, the *Daoine Sidhe* ("theena shee"), who are of human size or larger; they are beautiful, passionate, noble, skilled in warfare, poetry, and music. Alongside them live the *cluricaune* and the *lepracaun,* squat little Paddy types who enjoy whiskey, tobacco, singing coarse songs, and hiding their gold. Even the Irish mermen, the *merrows,* display national characteristics: "[They] appear as fish-men with green teeth and hair and short finny arms. Their eyes are like those of a pig, and they have red noses from perpetual drinking."[2] The Scandinavian *tomte* and *nisse* specialize in agriculture and horseplay, the Italian *folletti* in the pursuit of women. Identification and mockery of national characteristics, though an ancient human pastime, is now generally taboo even in private conversation; perhaps that is why it emerged, as suppressed topics so often do, in "children's" literature. (Works like the *Field Guide,* though published as juveniles, are not of course only intended for or bought for — let alone by — children.*)

The most popular sacred text of the fairy faith, on the *New York Times* best-seller list for more than a year in the late 1970s and for many weeks number one, was a book called

---

*The *Field Guide,* for one thing, is full of uncensored sexual and scatalogical material.

Gnomes (1977), by Wil Huygen. This volume, still in print and selling well, is a very large, handsome picture book, first published in the Netherlands as *Leven en Weken de Kabouter* and, though bought largely by adults, presented as juvenile nonfiction. The gnomes' daily life, houses, dress, diet, crafts, sports, and social structure are described exactly as if they were Indians or Eskimos. Every page is richly illustrated in color by Rien Poortvliet, a well-known Dutch artist. The text, though translated from the Dutch by a group of anonymous, possibly imaginary, beings whose names the publisher does not choose to reveal, is lively and interesting. The translation of *kabouter* as "gnome," however, is in error. Gnomes, in folk tradition, live far underground, usually in mountain caves, where they mine and guard the treasures of the earth; their natures, appropriately, are flinty and taciturn. The *kabouter* (German *Kobold*) is the equivalent of the English brownie or pixie.

Most of *Gnomes* is original rather than based on folklore, which has little to say about the private lives of the solitary or household fairies. Poortvliet and Huygen's gnomes are domestic and good-natured; they are only about six inches tall (much smaller than the traditional gnome or *tomte*) and live for eight hundred years. They build cozy peasant chalets under the roots of oak trees and spend their days farming, gathering wild foods (they are vegetarians), befriending animals and birds, and practicing simple crafts like basketry, pottery, leather working, and carpentry. They do folk dances and sing folk songs, drink herbal teas and homemade wine, and practice herbal medicine and acupuncture.

For the American reader, at least, *Gnomes* represented the countercultural life-style of the sixties, which by 1979 had literally gone underground. Instead of dropping out of urban society and moving to the country to set up an ideal self-sufficient community, like the previous generation, the readers of *Gnomes* fantasized about such an adventure. The book also has a strong ecological moral, which becomes explicit at the end when a wise, elderly gnome named Tomte Haroldson, who once knew Mozart and Rembrandt, visits the author and the illustrator. He tells them that mankind must learn to honor its artists, stop destroying and polluting the world, and live in harmony with nature again as the gnomes do.

All this is harmless and even admirable, probably better for its readers than *Mad* magazine or Spider-Man comics. Unfortunately, the book has a less nice side: it is politically neoconservative and extraordinarily sexist. Most of the gnomes so charmingly pictured are male, and so are all the interesting gnomic occupations and adventures. Males alone wear the colorful traditional costume and red cap, and all crafts except spinning and weaving are their exclusive province. Male gnomes design and build the houses, practice medicine and farming, and rule the family. The male gnome does the courting; the female, who looks like a fat blond Dutch doll with very large pink breasts ("Plump womenfolk, round of form, are the favorites"[3]), waits to be courted. After marriage she stays at home cooking and minding the children. "Mainly because of the gray color of her clothing, the female gnome feels safer indoors";[4] outside she might be mistaken for a mouse by some predator. In which case, no doubt, it would be her own fault, as is sometimes said of rape victims. Even in her own domain patriarchy is plainly in evidence: the only artworks on the walls of the gnome house are carved sculptures of two famous ancestors — both male.

As for politics, gnomes live in a benevolent monarchy, ruled by a king. Social conformity seems to be universal and creative expression almost unknown (in spite of Tomte Haroldson's patronage of Mozart). Most gnome households own only one book, the "Secret Book," which is read aloud (by the father, naturally) on special occasions.

Perhaps made greedily hasty by the runaway success of *Gnomes,* its publishers rushed into print a companion volume entitled *Faeries* (1978).[5] This work is not, like its predecessor, a loving and imaginative account of a single species, but yet another hodgepodge compendium of goblins, elves, ogres, et cetera. The archaic spelling of the title may have been adopted to reassure prospective buyers that the book had nothing to do with deviance — a reassurance that was possibly ill founded. Unlike *Gnomes, Faeries* does not celebrate the nuclear patriarchal family but suggests — especially in its illustrations — a world of haunting and ambiguous sexuality. It is full of leering dwarfs and hags and of naked and lovely, barely pubescent or prepubescent winged girls and boys, some without even a scrap of thistledown or a helpful butterfly to cover their private parts.

The watercolors that illustrate *Faeries,* by the brilliant young English artists Brian Froud and Alan Lee, are beautifully done if derivative. They are a remarkable amalgam of Arthur Rackham, Edmund Dulac, Richard Dadd, John Henry Fuseli, and every other gifted English painter of the supernatural you can, consciously or unconsciously, recall — by turns beautiful, grotesque, comic, and terrifying. The book as a whole, however, seems to have been put together overnight by a committee. There is no apparent order or plan to it, and the text is shamefully derivative. Although no credit is given, most of *Faeries* appears to have been lifted outright from the works of the eminent British folklorist Katharine Briggs (1898–1980). If "faeries" really did exist, as this book pretends, those responsible for its publication would be in serious trouble. The Good Folk, though themselves sometimes light-fingered, dislike thieves; and if certain Abrams executives have suffered over the past decade from unaccountable painful twinges and pinching sensations in their arms and legs, or found their material gains (symbolically, perhaps) turned into toadstools and dead leaves, they will know why.

Katharine Briggs's own compendia of fairy lore are models of responsible scholarship. Her widely praised *Encyclopedia of Fairies* (1976) is an impressive and also an entrancing book. Besides many folktales, it includes not only entries for every sort of magical being found in the British Isles but also ones for general topics such as "Changelings" and "Fairy Food" and for the best-known writers on the faiⅼies, from John Aubrey to W. B. Yeats. It is also well indexed by type and motif according to the standard system used by all folklorists. I am delighted to say that it is still in print. Briggs's *The Vanishing People* (1978) is equally scholarly; it is a study of beliefs about the fairies not only in England and Ireland but on the Continent. Briggs discusses, most entertainingly, such matters as the supernatural passage of time in fairyland, fairy sports, and theories of the origin of the fairies — both simple and sophisticated. Are they the ghosts of the dead, diminished gods and nature spirits, or memories of an earlier race of small, dark people who lived in mound dwellings (fairy hills) and feared iron? She makes an interesting case for all these theories, pointing out where one explanation is most likely or where another isn't.

Dr. Briggs, a former president of the English Folklore Society and holder of both a D. Phil. and D. Litt. from Oxford, probably knew more about hobgoblins, brownies, and bogies than anyone now living; she was the author of the classic *The Anatomy of Puck* (1959), which deals with fairy lore in Shakespeare and his contemporaries; and also of two first-rate stories for children, *Kate Crackernuts* (1963) and *Hobberdy Dick* (1955), a tale about a household brownie remarkable for its faithfulness to tradition. But her lifework was certainly the *Dictionary of British Folk Tales in the English Language* (1970–71), a four-volume encyclopedia that reprints or summarizes all the fairy tales, novellas, animal stories, fables, and legends collected in the British Isles — including many hitherto available only in manuscript. This monumental work is thoroughly researched, elegantly printed, and completely annotated and indexed. It is a fine source for scholars of many sorts; moreover, it is fascinating to read — the perfect bedside book.*

Today, the fascination with folklore, especially on the part of young people, continues — though in a moderated form and with emphasis on folktales and popular legends rather than on the ethnography of the supernatural. What is the reason for this preoccupation? Possibly it is a by-product of the overly material and commercial world we live in: the result of an imaginatively deprived childhood.

Many of my students at Cornell, though they come from prosperous backgrounds, have grown up with no better nourishment for their imaginations than the crude comedy and plastic adventure stories of films and television: Disney and *Star Trek* instead of Pooh and *Treasure Island*. They know the classics of children's literature only in cheap cartoon versions, if at all.

But often, in late adolescence, such readers discover books like *The Hobbit* and *The Wind in the Willows* and Grimms' fairy tales. They take possession of a fantasy world that should have been theirs at eight or ten, with the intellectual enthusiasm, the romantic eagerness — and the purchasing power — of eighteen and twenty. From among them come the mind-blown customers for "Come to Middle Earth" posters and Pooh T-shirts; of collections of folktales and guides to gnomes and fairies.

Throughout history, when God appears to be dead or

---

*The complete set is for expensive bedsides only; but a good one-volume selection appeared in 1977 as *British Folktales*.

sleeping, the elves and bogies come out to play. Some of us welcome them because they are more amusing and less threatening. They may bring us good and bad luck — make our vegetable gardens flourish, help us find lost objects, lead us astray in a fog, give us rheumatic twinges or bad dreams — but they will never judge us. Most of them are smaller than we are, and even if their wills are bent on malice, their power is limited to certain places and times. Best of all, they are not responsible for the mess our world is in.

5

The Child Who Followed
the Piper

KATE GREENAWAY

One of the gifts an artist may have is the ability to create
what J.R.R. Tolkien called a "secondary world" — a fully
imagined alternate universe, as consistent as our own or
possibly more so. Such a secondary world may make visible
some aspect of the primary one, so that once we have seen,
for instance, a landscape by Corot, a play by Chekhov, or a
film by Chaplin, we will find echoes of it ever after.

Not all artists have this gift. Some painters of the first
rank lack it, while some of the second rank are given it in
abundance. It can even coexist with a level of skill that would
keep its possessor out of most galleries today. Kate Greenaway, who was famous in her own time for her pictures of
pretty children in pastoral landscapes, is hardly visible when
measured against the best artists of her period. She began
her career as, and in many ways remained, a designer of
greeting cards. Her color sense was refined but timid, her
range of subjects narrow. As a draftsman she was at times
almost pathetic: her trees seem to be made of green sponge,
her sheep look like poodles, and even John Ruskin, her greatest fan, could not teach her perspective. All she could really

draw was flowers and children, especially good little girls —
and even here she sometimes faltered: Ruskin irascibly described the feet of her figures as "shapeless paddles or flap-
pers."[1] Yet she was as popular in her own time, and is
probably better known today, than either Randolph Caldecott
or Walter Crane, the other members of the trio that revo-
lutionized the picture book in the late nineteenth century —
though Crane was a better graphic designer and Caldecott a
superior draftsman.

Outwardly Kate Greenaway seems in no way a subversive artist. Yet her little boys and girls are far freer than
most middle-class children in Victorian England, when well-
to-do children, especially girls, wore heavy, stiff, uncom-
fortable clothing and were almost never observed running
barefoot on the grass. Greenaway's world was also completely rural and preindustrial; it can be seen as a silent protest
against what the railways and the factories were doing to the
English countryside and the towns.

Kate Greenaway's work is also subversive in another,
less obvious sense — one that most of her readers might
never have noticed and of which she was probably unaware
herself. Underneath the innocent surfaces of her drawings
and rhymes there occasionally appears a kind of sentimental
sensuality about childhood that was one of the darker secrets
of the Victorian age and that, as we shall see, brought her
at least one dubious admirer.

THE CLASSIC makers of children's literature are not usually
men and women who had consistently happy childhoods —
or consistently unhappy ones. Rather they are those whose
early happiness ended suddenly and often disastrously. Char-
acteristically, they lost one or both parents early. They were
abruptly shunted from one home to another, like Louisa May
Alcott, Kenneth Grahame, and Mark Twain — or even, like

Frances Hodgson Burnett, E. Nesbit, and J.R.R. Tolkien, from one continent to another. L. Frank Baum and Lewis Carroll were sent away to harsh and bullying schools; Rudyard Kipling was taken from India to England by his affectionate but ill-advised parents and left in the care of stupid and brutal strangers. Cheated of their full share of childhood, these men and women later re-created, and transfigured, their lost worlds. Though she was primarily an artist rather than a writer, Kate Greenaway belongs in this company.

In the more than eighty years since Kate Greenaway's death there have been only two biographies of her. The first, M. H. Spielmann and G. S. Layard's *Kate Greenaway* (1905), is a rambling, lavishly illustrated, eulogistic whitewash, which does its best to make her into one of her own quaint, old-fashioned figures. Rodney Engen's serious and perceptive study, published in 1981, was long overdue. As he shows, Greenaway's childhood, in the classic pattern, was marked by turbulence and sudden deprivation.

Though Kate Greenaway was born in London, when she was eight months old her mother became ill, and Kate was put out to nurse on a farm in Nottinghamshire. Kate called the farmer's wife, Mary Chappell, "Maman" and wrote of her later as "the kindest, most generous, most charitable, the cheerfulest and most careful woman"[2] she had ever known. "In all things she was highest and best."[3] No description by Kate of her real mother has survived; she is said to have had a "stern, religious nature . . . resolved to do what was, in her view, morally right."[4]

After two years in the country, Kate was brought back to gray, grimy, working-class Victorian London, where her father, a wood engraver, was struggling with decreasing success to support his increasing family. When Kate was five the family moved again, to Islington, and her mother opened a small shop selling children's and ladies' dresses and trimmings. It prospered, but Mrs. Greenaway was now at work from eight A.M. till eight P.M., and the care of Kate and her younger sister and brother was transferred to twelve-year-old Lizzie, the eldest child. Since their house had no yard or garden, the four children spent most of their time wandering about the London streets. In the summer, when there was enough money to spare, they would be sent to Nottinghamshire, and Kate would stay with the Chappells in what she always insisted was her real home.

Unlike the little girls in her books, Kate Greenaway was an odd, awkward, plain child — intensely shy, strong-willed, and moody. When she was sent to school she had trembling fits that lasted for days, or until she was removed; as a result, she was educated largely at home. She was subject to recurrent nightmares, including one in which her father's face would change to that of a stranger; "she would desperately tear off the false face, only to be confronted by another and yet another, but never his own."[5] The prospect of becoming an adult held no attraction for her: as she wrote later, "I hated to be grown-up, and cried when I had my first long dress."[6]

Kate Greenaway's skill at drawing persuaded her parents to send her to art school when she was twelve. She was a docile and dedicated student who made few friends and won prizes for delicate, carefully executed, academically correct work. She went on to become a moderately successful but undistinguished commercial artist, whose greeting-card designs and magazine illustrations clearly derived from the best-known figures of the time: Walter Crane, Richard Dadd, and Sir John Tenniel. The breakthrough did not come until she was thirty-two, when she began *Under the Window*, a collection of verses and drawings in what was to become her famous and characteristic manner. The book was published for Christmas, 1879, and was an instant popular success.

What Kate Greenaway had done was to imagine and

portray a world that thousands of people then and since have
wanted to enter in imagination. Her vision was of an idealized
childhood in an idealized English country landscape: of sweet
babies and delicately pretty girls and boys playing in perfectly
tended gardens, gathering flowers in cow pie–free meadows,
and dancing on the tidy village green. In the Greenaway world
it seldom rains and is nearly always springtime or summer;
everyone is graceful, charming, and prettily dressed. Though
her books appeared in the 1870s and 1880s, her figures usually wear the styles of Wordsworth's time rather than her
own — the simple loose frocks and smocks and slippers of
the ideal Romantic child. These quaint, old-fashioned cos-
tumes are appropriate, since what Kate Greenaway presents
is a greeting-card version of Wordsworthian innocence, untouched by age, dirt, poverty, illness, care, or sin. Ultimately,
perhaps, her vision derives from William Blake, particularly
from the illustrations to his *Songs of Innocence,* many of which
show an ideal rural scene peopled by children in loose, light-
colored clothes.[7]

Though the popularity of Kate Greenaway's world
seems easy to understand, in fact it has certain odd aspects
that are not apparent at first glance. For one thing, there
is the extreme, almost obsessive attention to costume.
The clothes her children wear were often sewn for her
models by her own hands, and details of construction and
trim are so carefully noted that they could be — and sometimes have been — reproduced as if from a fashion plate.
Possibly we should expect this from someone who was the
daughter of a ladies' milliner and outfitter — and also from
someone who, disliking her own appearance, wore drab,
dowdy clothes. Other factors must be responsible for the
strange air of disengagement and even melancholy that often
hangs over her scenes. Greenaway children are as a whole
remarkably quiet and well behaved. They seldom quarrel or

fight; they smile infrequently and almost never laugh or cry. Even when they are playing together they do not seem to be much aware of one another; their habitual expression is one of dreamy self-absorption. The only close relationships occur between mother and child, or between an older girl and smaller children.

Another odd thing about Kate Greenaway's world is that most of the people in it are young and female. She shows a few old ladies, but not many women between twenty and sixty. And — except in *The Pied Piper of Hamelin,* of which more later — there are almost no males over the age of ten. Moreover, the little boys are greatly outnumbered by the little girls, and those who do appear are often rather girlish-looking.

A fantasy world populated largely by sweet, pretty, charmingly dressed, dreamily innocent little girls was well suited to the Victorian cult of the child — especially the female child. The preference for childishness and innocence in adult females was widespread, and some Victorians carried it to the point of preferring actual little girls to grown women. This taste might be expressed harmlessly in friendship, as in the case of Lewis Carroll. Or it might become overtly and destructively sexual, as Steven Marcus has shown in *The Other Victorians.* Kate Greenaway's most famous fan, John Ruskin, seems to have fallen between these two extremes. The story of his disastrous, unconsummated marriage to Effie Gray and his thwarted love for the neurasthenic Rose La Touche is too well known to need retelling here; but it is worth recalling that Effie was thirteen years old when Ruskin first became interested in her, and Rose nine, and that they were both physically very much the Greenaway type. Ruskin himself had been deprived of his full share of childhood happiness, and in a more thoroughgoing way than Kate had. As a child prodigy, he was allowed no playmates and almost no toys by his puritanical but obsessively devoted mother; most of his time was spent in lessons or in solitary contemplation.

In 1879, when *Under the Window* was published, Ruskin was sixty, "a weary, broken man, famed throughout Britain for his books and lectures, but plagued by fits of madness triggered by overwork."[8] He had resigned his professorship at Oxford and retired to his country house in Lancashire, "where he received a steady stream of well-wishers and maintained a voluminous correspondence with his admirers, particularly young, unmarried women. . . . his 'pets' as he called them."[9] Another favorite activity was having little girls from the local parish school to tea. The dainty nymphet charm of Greenaway's figures was almost guaranteed to appeal to Ruskin, who, as he put it, wanted only to be loved "as a child loves."[10] His enthusiasm for *Under the Window* was immediate; and shortly after it appeared he wrote Kate Greenaway a long letter in a highly playful and somewhat feverish tone:

> My dear Miss Greenaway — I lay awake half (no a quarter) of last night thinking of the hundred things I want to say to you — and never shall get said! — and I'm giddy and weary — and now can't say even half or a quarter of one out of the hundred. They're about you — and your gifts — and your graces — and your fancies — and your — yes — perhaps one or two little tiny faults: — and about other people — children, and grey-haired, and what you could do for them — if you once made up your mind for whom you would do it. For children only for instance? — or for old people, me for instance — [11]

What Kate Greenaway could do for Ruskin soon became evident. He was still haunted by the memory of Rose La Touche, who had died four years earlier, and, as Rodney Engen points out, "*Under the Window* abounded in suggestive images: drawings of pink roses, bowls of rose blossoms, a girl in a pale frock clutching a bouquet of roses ('Will you be my little wife, If I ask you? Do!')."[12] He wanted original drawings, sketches, and watercolors of pretty young "girlies" (his term), the more of them the better. For the rest of his life Kate recognized this need and kept Ruskin supplied with what an unsympathetic modern critic might describe as soft-core kiddie porn — though Ruskin's public position was that her drawings expressed an almost spiritual ideal: "The radiance and innocence of re-instated infant divinity showered again among the flowers of English meadows."[13] Apparently he never repaid Kate Greenaway for any of these gifts, some of which took days to complete — though he was a rich man and she an overworked artist struggling to support not only herself but her parents.

All pornography, even of the most rarefied and decorous kind, appears to be subject to a law of diminishing returns. After a while a new and slightly different version of the same stimulus is necessary in order to produce the desired response. If this were not so, one copy of *Hustler* would last its purchaser a lifetime, and most of the shops in Times Square would be out of business. The pictures of pretty "girlies" that Kate Greenaway sent to Ruskin aroused almost embarrassing raptures of appreciation, but more were always wanted. If he thought only of himself, he once wrote, "I could contentedly and proudly keep you drawing nicest girls in blue sashes with soft eyes and blissful lips, to the end of my poor bit of life."[14] Even the most delightful of her figures, however, seemed to Ruskin to have one fault: they were overdressed. He wrote to her persistently on this topic: "Will you — (it's all for your own good — !) make her stand up and then draw her for me without a cap — and, without her shoes, — (because of the heels) and without her mittens, and without her — frock and frills? And let me see exactly how tall she is — and — how — round. It will be so good of and for you — And to and for me."[15] But Kate Greenaway was deeply prim; she might spend days working on a gift for Ruskin, but she refused to undress her figures.

Though his need for Kate's drawings was private, Ruskin's enthusiasm for her work soon became public. In a lecture at Oxford in 1883 he spoke of her "genius" and "tried to convince his amazed audience that Kate ranked among the most important of old master and contemporary artists."[16] To understand the effect of this we must imagine someone like Sir Kenneth Clark speaking at Harvard on the genius of Norman Rockwell. Privately, Ruskin went even further: writing to thank her for a hand-painted Christmas card, he remarked, "To my mind it is a greater thing than Raphael's St. Cecilia."[17]

At other times and in other mental states Ruskin was quite aware that Kate Greenaway was not the equal of Raphael. He took on the task of correcting her "little tiny faults"[18] and directing her artistic career as he had in the past, unsuccessfully, tried to direct those of other artists, among them J.M.W. Turner, Dante Gabriel Rossetti, John Millais, and Edward Burne-Jones. In Kate Greenaway's case he was no more successful, but he was more readily obeyed. He complained of the clumsiness of her drawing and demanded that she make detailed realistic copies of plants, rocks, and domestic objects ("When are you going to be good and send me a study of . . . the coalscuttle or the dust pan — or a towel or a clothes screen — "[19]). She accepted his criticisms humbly and carried out his assignments conscientiously, but without any noticeable effect on her published work. The studies she did for Ruskin are largely without interest and show that his dedicated scolding had succeeded only in temporarily turning a gifted professional illustrator into a mediocre and conventional Victorian art student. Fortunately, Kate

Greenaway was wise enough not to abandon the style and the subjects that had made her famous.

Patrons of porn shops are notoriously unwilling to make eye contact with the proprietor, let alone to form a close acquaintance, and Ruskin showed a similar reluctance to meet Kate Greenaway. Though he wrote to her as "Sweetest Katie" and signed his letters "loving J.R.," it took him two years to propose a meeting. Before he came to tea in her studio Kate Greenaway was so nervous she almost wished she had not invited him; but the visit was a great success, and from then until his death he was the most important person in her life.

In 1883 Ruskin was sixty-three, and to the disinterested observer a person of no particular charm. Beatrix Potter, who met him a year or so later, described him in her diary as a "ridiculous figure," untidily dressed and "not particularly clean looking"[20] — in other words, a dirty old man. Nevertheless, he had many female admirers of all ages, and he soon also became the focus of Kate Greenaway's affections. She was deeply flattered and excited by Ruskin's praise, thrilled by the intimate, playful tone of his letters and conversations, and awed by the willingness of this famous man to consider her as a friend and a pupil. As Rodney Engen shows, she was soon thoroughly in love and regarded Ruskin with an almost religious reverence. Men like him, she wrote to another friend, were "far above and beyond ordinary people," and she hoped that "whilst I possess life I may venerate and admire with unstinted admiration, this sort of noble and great men."[21] After she had spent a month visiting Ruskin in the country, she confided to his cousin, Joan Severn, "Words can hardly say the sort of man he is — perfect — simply."[22]

Ruskin, on the other hand, was in love with Kate's work, not with Kate herself. She was no graceful Greenaway "girlie," but a plain, dumpy, dowdy spinster of thirty-six, with a working-class background, a shy, nervous manner, and a pronounced lisp. The resulting tragicomedy was of a sort familiar to all painters and writers who do not have the good fortune to be as handsome, charming, and eloquent as their work. This happens fairly often, since many — perhaps most — artists are partly motivated by a wish to create something superior to themselves. As a result, fans who meet them for the first time often feel a pang of disappointment, expressed in remarks like "He was smaller than/older than/ fatter than I thought he'd be" or "She didn't say anything all that interesting."

The relationship between Ruskin and Kate Greenaway was an uneven one in both senses. He lectured and teased, praised and criticized; he asked her to stay with him in the country and then withdrew the invitation; he promised to visit her studio and then made flimsy excuses not to, or came only briefly and spent all his time there flirting with her child models. As Engen puts it, "He wanted attention, but on his own terms; while he urged her to write often, he stressed the importance of his own silence."[23]

Rodney Engen, like most biographers, is a partisan of his subject, and he indignantly accuses Ruskin of having "played a cruel game with Kate's emotions; his letters encouraged her with lavish praises; then, when she became too affectionate, he became cool and turned away from her."[24] This, on the evidence given, does not seem quite accurate. Ruskin's treatment of Kate Greenaway was cruel, but it was not a deliberate game: rather it was the result of his mental instability, his recurring attacks of depression and his constant fear of madness. Kate apparently did not understand how precarious his mental health was or why, when he would not come to see her, he remained in contact with other — usually younger, prettier, and less emotionally exhausting — admirers. In fact Ruskin, though flattered, was also embarrassed and perhaps even frightened by the intensity of Kate's feelings for him, and by the alternately demanding and pleading tone of her letters. "My dear Kate," he wrote in 1886, "There is not the remotest chance or possibility of you or any-body else in London seeing me this year and if you begin snewsing [*sic*] and probing again — I close correspondence on the instant. . . . You ought to have known my heart world is dead — long ago."[25]

A definite rejection like this certainly might have made Kate Greenaway's life easier, if it had been consistently main-tained; but Ruskin, unbalanced as he was and eager for her drawings, blew hot and cold. Sometimes he refused even to open Kate's letters; a few weeks or months later he might write to her so warmly and intimately that all her hopes would revive. Like Kate's father in her childhood nightmare, he showed her first one false face and then another.

It was during this period that Kate Greenaway began to write a series of awkward and often unfinished but deeply felt love poems, of which only a few have ever been published. Her first biographers print several of these verses, while assuring the reader that they had nothing to do with Kate's life; rather it merely "pleased and soothed her to work out a poetic problem. . . . The case was not her own."[26] Rodney Engen, who takes the opposite view, seems to be nearer to the truth. The poems do not suggest someone who is pleased and soothed:

> Nothing to do but part dear
> Oh love love love, my heart
> Is slowly breaking and coldness creeping
> Nearer into my every part.[27]

During this same period of emotional turmoil Kate Greenaway produced her two most unusual books. The first one, *A Apple Pie,* published in the fall of 1886, was much larger in format than most of her work, and the figures were also larger and more active. Perhaps significantly, the drawings had never been submitted for Ruskin's approval, though she usually consulted him about all her major work. The Mother Goose rhyme she had chosen to illustrate describes the struggles of a group of alphabetically named individuals (in her pictures, mainly little girls) for the possession of what she shows as an outsize pie.

A   apple pie
B   bit it
C   cut it
.   .   .   .
F   fought for it
G   got it
H   had it
J   jumped for it
K   knelt for it[28]

In the traditional versions, K either "kept it" or "kicked it."[29] That Kate should make this change suggests that she felt herself to be in a one-down position, having to beg for what she wanted.

It may not be too farfetched to view this large pie as John Ruskin, and the children as his various "pets" and admirers competing for a share of his attention as they so often did — and in the end literally eating him up. Whether or not Ruskin got the message, his reaction to *A Apple Pie* was very hostile. According to Engen, "he considered the project a personal affront, an insult to their friendship"[30] and wrote Kate Greenaway a series of scathingly critical letters. In fact, *A Apple Pie* is one of Kate Greenaway's most attractive books; it has a boldness of design and energy of execution that are missing in much of her work.

The next uncharacteristic Greenaway project, *The Pied*

Piper of Hamelin (1888), was undertaken with Ruskin's approval and under his supervision. He approved of her plan to illustrate Robert Browning's poem, adopting for the purpose a somewhat Pre-Raphaelite style and a palette dominated by rust, ocher, and olive tones instead of her usual pastels. He sent her copies of his favorite paintings as models, and also exercises in perspective which she carried out conscientiously but without noticeable result.

To illustrate any text is also to interpret it, and Kate Greenaway's *The Pied Piper* is an excellent example of this process. In Browning's poem the Piper is an eccentric trickster figure, "tall and thin, / With sharp blue eyes, each like a pin."[31] Greenaway pictures him as a kind of romantic hero: pale, dignified, melancholy, and mysterious, with a resemblance to portraits of Ruskin that can hardly be accidental. (The echo between the titles of these two books — Pie / Pied Piper — may be mere coincidence. It might be noted, however, that Kate Greenaway had already thought of illustrating Browning's poem in 1885 and had written to him for permission to do so. In this case it would be the Piper who turned into a pie, and not vice versa — which makes more sense.)

As Browning tells it, *The Pied Piper* is a moral fable. The burghers of Hamelin hire the Piper to charm away the rats that are plaguing the town, but once the rats have been drowned in the river they refuse to pay him. In revenge he plays a different tune, which draws all the children of Hamelin skipping and dancing after him. This enchanted procession (consisting, by my count, of 128 girls and only 46 boys) follows the Piper out of town and into a mountain crevice that supernaturally opens to receive them. Browning never reports what was inside the mountain. One child who was too lame to keep up with the rest says later that they were promised "a joyous land . . . Where waters gushed and fruit-trees grew, / And flowers put forth a fairer hue";[32] but of course these promises may have been as illusory as the visions of tripe and pickles with which the Piper lured the rats to their doom. The final lines of the poem provide a matter-of-fact moral:

> So, Willy, let me and you be wipers
> Of scores out with all men — especially pipers![33]

Kate Greenaway's illustrations, however, make good on the Piper's promises. She added a final scene, reproduced as the frontispiece and cover of her book, which shows the Pied Piper sitting and playing in a springtime orchard while beautiful Greenaway children dance round a tree and others embrace him. Ruskin, who followed this project closely, "supervised her work on this one scene with unswerving dedication," and he later wrote, "Yes, that is just what it must be, the piper sitting in the garden playing. It perfects the whole story, while it changes it into a new one."[34] He tried to get her to undress at least some of the children — "I think we might go the length of expecting the frocks to come off sometimes"[35] — but Kate, as usual, ignored this hint. She did, however, follow Ruskin's instructions in substituting flimsy white dresses and wreaths of flowers for the heavier, darker clothes in which the children had left Hamelin. So the "new story" was made to end with the Piper surrounded by beautiful girlies in what Ruskin called the "paradise scene"[36] and said represented his idea of heaven. Kate, in this story, is nowhere — though perhaps we are to imagine her as the feminine-looking lame boy left outside the mountain.

The Pied Piper, in this view, would represent a final act of self-sacrifice on Kate's part: an acceptance of the fact that there was no place for her in Ruskin's life except as the provider of images that might comfort him and lift him out of his increasing melancholy. But she was denied even this satisfaction. As Ruskin's mental condition worsened, even her drawings did not always cheer him up; sometimes they seemed only a painful reminder of how much he had lost. When she begged for news, he asked if she realized how sad he always was, "how the pain and failure of age torment me — what an agony of longing there is in me for the days of youth — of childhood — here every one of your drawings is as of heaven into which I can never enter — ?"[37] Gradually, as he sank into the depression and confusion of his final years, he broke off relations with her completely.

Kate Greenaway's own poems suggest that eventually she realized that her idealized great man was an illusion:

The You I loved was my creation — mine,
    Without a counterpart within yourself.
I gave you thoughts and soul and heart
    Taken from Love's ideal.[38]

But she never abandoned Ruskin; during the nine years of silence before his death she continued to write to him and to send him drawings and watercolors.

For Kate Greenaway too the last years of the century and of her life (she died in 1901) were hard ones. She was lonely and often ill, and her drawings were going out of fashion in a world that had discovered Aubrey Beardsley and the Impressionists. Yet she had, and still has, her passionate supporters. Many of her books remain in print today, and nice little girls all over the Western world can be seen wearing versions of the styles she made famous. To the general public she is probably much better known than John Ruskin. Even the most major criticism is time-bound and speaks mainly to its own contemporaries; but the most minor work of art, if it creates a true secondary world, can seem as fresh after a century as on the day it was made.

6

Tales of Terror

MRS. CLIFFORD

Odd and psychologically disturbing passages are not uncommon in Victorian children's books. Even the works of writers like Lewis Carroll and George MacDonald contain characters and happenings that might haunt an older reader, let alone a child. Often such books reveal wishes and fears that are denied or disguised in adult literature. Lucy Lane Clifford's *Anyhow Stories* (1882), though virtually unknown today except by reputation, is such a book. Some of its tales, notably "The New Mother" and "Wooden Tony"[1] are almost classically full of pity and terror.

In her own time Mrs. Clifford was a successful novelist and dramatist, the author of several best-sellers, and the hostess of a London literary salon. She knew George Eliot, Rudyard Kipling, Henry James, James Russell Lowell, and many other writers. Born Lucy Lane in Barbados, she came to London to study art and in 1875 married William Kingdon Clifford, a gifted young professor of mathematics and the friend of Thomas Huxley, George Henry Lewes, and Leslie Stephen. But after only four years Clifford died, leaving his wife with two young daughters and very little money. George Eliot helped her to get a Civil List pension, which she began to supplement almost at once by writing: romantic novels, verse, plays, and short stories.

Like so many other women writers of her time, Mrs. Clifford wrote both for love and money. At first her principal motive was to keep the pot boiling, and much of what she produced was the standard Victorian and Edwardian stew of romance, melodrama, high-mindedness, and high life, spiced with just enough passion to titillate but not actually shock the reader. But even in her worst books there are passages of good writing, and her best novel, *Aunt Anne,* well deserves the praise it received from her friend Henry James, who often addressed Mrs. Clifford in his letters as "Aunt Lucy."

Aunt Anne (1892) is a psychological study of the sort James might well have admired. The eponymous heroine is a sixtyish spinster who is both sentimental and calculating, weak and determined. The story of how, under cover of family affection, she moves in on her nephew Walter and his wife, forcing them to support her extravagances and alter their life-style to suit hers, is comedy almost worthy of Jane Austen. But the remainder of the novel has darker undertones. Aunt Anne gradually becomes involved with a young fortune hunter, the sinister and pathetic Alfred Wimple: "To look at he was not prepossessing; he had a pinky complexion, pale reddish hair and small round dark eyes with light lashes and weak lids. . . . He was fairly gentleman-like, but only fairly so, and he did not look very agreeable. . . . The oddest thing about him was that with all his unprepossessing appearance he had a certain air of sentiment."[2]

Mrs. Clifford's account of this relationship, and of the deceptions Aunt Anne and Wimple practice on each other, themselves, and their friends and relations, is Jamesian in its subtlety and elaboration. It would be interesting to know how much of this novel was written in deliberate or unconscious imitation of Henry James. Certainly Aunt Anne has something

in common with Miss Tina in *The Aspern Papers* (1888), also
a ridiculous, pathetic, provincial old woman who falls in love
with a much younger man.

Anyhow Stories contains tales Mrs. Clifford had evidently told
to her own daughters; in "The New Mother" the protagonists
are even called by her children's nicknames, Turkey and Blue-
Eyes. The book is uneven: some of the stories and verses
are conventionally sentimental and moral, pale copies of the
work of then-popular juvenile authors like Mrs. Molesworth;
others are startlingly original.

Especially interesting to a modern reader is the psychological sophistication of the best of these tales. Many of
Mrs. Clifford's characters have the mechanical sense of the
world and precarious relation to reality that we now associate
with schizophrenia. In "The Imitation Fish," which suggests
the fairy tales of Hans Christian Andersen, a tin toy fish lives
in dread "lest its falseness should be betrayed"[3] to the child
whom it loves. Instead, something even worse happens: the
child, believing the fish real, throws it away into the sea.

Fish seem somehow to be associated with unreality for
Mrs. Clifford; in the poem "The Paper Ship" the narrator
sails "away in a paper ship,"

> Away on an unknown sea;
> And all the fishes were hollow, my dear,
> And all of them swam at me.

He travels to a nightmare land where all the people are
dolls:

> The town was built of card and paint,
> The gardens were made of tin;
> And dolls looked out at the windows, dear,
> And all of them asked me in.

And dolls sat round on the chairs inside;
>   They all were dressed so fine;
They stared at a clock that never had ticked,
>   And was ever at half-past nine.

"What shall we do to be real?" they cried.
>   "What shall we do to be real?
We none of us feel, though we look so nice,
>   And talk of the vague ideal."[4]

Surely what is mocked here is the expenses and pretensions of London upper-class social life — as seen, perhaps, by children. It is a world where people are cold fish, unreal and hollow. The scene is a London drawing room; half past nine is the hour when guests would gather there after a dinner party.

"Wooden Tony" appears at first glance to be a fairy story about art in which a boy sings a wonderful song and becomes immortal. But just beneath it is the far stranger tale of a mentally troubled, possibly autistic child in a Swiss village, a boy with a "pale face and wide open eyes"[5] who sits on a stool by the door of his house and sings to himself, letting "the days and nights slip by as one that swims with but just enough movement to keep himself from drowning. So Tony seemed to swim through time."[6]

As the years pass Tony becomes unable to work and speaks less and less: a "great cobweb seemed to have wrapped him round,"[7] and he "lived among his dreams, which grew so tangled that even he could not tell the sleeping from the waking ones."[8] He grows more and more stiff and silent and at the end of the story is taken away to the city and becomes a wooden man, a figure on a kind of giant cuckoo clock — or, perhaps, a patient in an asylum: "He was in the darkness . . . all time was the same to him. . . . Hour after hour it was always the same, day after day, week after week, month after month, in light and dark, in heat and cold."[9] The terror the story produces is related to that we feel when seeing, or even just reading about, children or adults who believe themselves to have become inanimate objects or machines.

In "The New Mother," on the other hand, the frightening thing is that inanimate matter has become real. This tale draws on the primitive fear of objects that survives just below the surface in most of us — the suspicion that our new tennis racket or our old Toyota is secretly hostile, that the politician speaking on television is really a plastic replica. It is also, of course, a classic tale of separation anxiety, made more terrifying because it does not take place "in a faraway land, but [in] England with typical village, post office, household furnishings etc."*

The "strange wild-looking girl"[10] whom the children in "The New Mother" find sitting by the wayside claims that she lives in their village, but they have never seen her there before. She is sitting on a musical instrument called a peardrum, which, she tells them, she will play only for naughty children. This peardrum, in the accompanying illustration, is shaped very like a womb; so it is not surprising to hear the girl claim that when she plays it a little man and woman come out and dance together. "The little woman has heard a secret — she tells it while she dances."[11]

Naturally the children long to see this dance and learn this secret, so they go home and try hard to be naughty. Their mother, distressed, tells them that if they do not stop she will have to go away and leave them "and send home a new mother, with glass eyes and a wooden tail."[12] But the

*Sanjay Sircar, Humanities Research Centre, Australian National University, private communication. Sircar also compares "The New Mother" to Shirley Jackson's story "The Lottery" in its juxtaposition of the ordinary and the fantastic.

children keep on trying to be naughty, encouraged by the girl with the peardrum, who remarks to them that "the pleasure of goodness centres in itself; the pleasures of naughtiness are many and varied."[13]

Day after day the children become naughtier — but never quite naughty enough for the strange girl. They break furniture and crockery, throw the clock on the floor, and put out the fire. Finally they behave so badly that their mother leaves them — but even then they do not get their wish. The strange girl dances past their cottage, accompanied by an old man playing in a peculiar way on a flute and two dogs waltzing on their hind legs. " 'Oh, stop!' " the children cry, " 'and show us the little man and woman now.' "[14]

But the strange girl passes on, calling back to them: "Your new mother is coming. She is already on her way; but she only walks slowly, for her tail is rather long, . . . but she is coming, she is coming — coming — coming."[15] The procession disappears down the road, becoming "a dark misty object."

The children return to their disordered and deserted cottage to wait for night, and for the arrival of the new mother: "Suddenly, while they were sitting by the fire, they heard a sound as of something heavy being dragged along the ground outside, and then there was a loud and terrible knocking."[16] Turkey and Blue-Eyes bolt the door, but the new mother breaks it open with her tail. The children escape into the cold, dark forest, where they wander about like the famous Babes in the Wood, lonely and miserable.* At the end of the story they are still living there, longing to go home and see their real mother once again.

*I am also indebted to Sanjay Sircar of the Humanities Research Centre for this comparison.

And still the new mother stays in the little cottage, but the windows are closed and the doors are shut, and no one knows what the inside looks like. Now and then, when the darkness has fallen and the night is still, hand in hand Blue-Eyes and the Turkey creep up near to the home in which they once were so happy, and with beating hearts they watch and listen; sometimes a blinding flash comes through the window, and they know it is the light from the new mother's glass eyes, or they hear a strange muffled noise, and they know it is the sound of her wooden tail as she drags it along the floor.[17]

The figure of the new mother and the elemental terror aroused by her coming seem to belong to a more primitive world than that of the usual English folktale. They suggest the carved wooden images and superstitions of the voodoo cult, which Mrs. Clifford may have seen or heard of during her childhood in Barbados and recalled, perhaps not even consciously, many years later.

Readers of Henry James may feel a particular shiver of recognition as they read this story. Like *The Turn of the Screw,* written sixteen years later, it is the tale of two innocent children in late Victorian England who encounter a strange, attractive young woman who may be either a devil or a damned soul. She tempts them to disobedience, promising to reveal ambiguously sexual secrets, gradually leads them further and further into evil, and then disappears abruptly. It would be interesting to know whether James, when he wrote his famous ghost story, remembered his friend Lucy Clifford's strange and haunting tale for children.

7

Ford Madox Ford's
Fairy Tales

Once upon a time there was a large, pink-faced, yellow-haired man who liked to tell stories. All kinds of stories: adventure and spy thrillers, historical dramas, romances and fantasies, tales of war and personal reminiscence, social comedy and social criticism. Unfortunately he overdid it. Between the ages of eighteen and sixty-five he published eighty-one books, including four juveniles and thirty-two novels. Of the latter, one, *The Good Soldier,* is a masterpiece; four or five others come near it, and the rest vary from interesting to awful. Overproduction, especially of inferior work, is hard on an author's imagination and also on his public reputation. If Ford Madox Ford had told fewer stories, he might be better known today.

Ford wrote not only because he enjoyed it but because, in an increasingly desperate way, he had to. As Arthur Mizener says in his fine biography *The Saddest Story* (without which this essay could not have been written), Ford's life was a series of "financial crises that forced him to write too much journalism and popular fiction."[1] From about 1900 on he began to live on advances from publishers for books he had often not yet finished or even begun, writing against time to earn money already spent.

Ford's books for children were written at the start of his career, before the economic pressure on him had become heavy, when his energy was high and his creative impulse strong. His first two fairy tales appeared when he was only eighteen, and the third before his twenty-first birthday. *Christina's Fairy Book* was not published until 1906, but most of the stories and verses it contains were probably composed sometime earlier.

Though Ford's fairy tales are subversive, they are so only in a very private way. They are, internal evidence suggests, family romances: wish-fulfilling fantasies, or disguised versions of his real life in which his sister and his future wife star as the heroines and his other relatives play various roles.

The Brown Owl, Ford's first published work, which came out in September 1892,[2] is a remarkable achievement for someone of his age. It began as a story told to his sister, Juliet, who was then ten years old. Later he wrote it down and showed it to his grandfather Ford Madox Brown, the well-known Pre-Raphaelite painter. Brown "was so delighted that he immediately made two illustrations for it, bullied Edward Garnett into seeing that Fisher Unwin published it, and rushed copies to all his friends."[3] The book was favorably noticed in several London newspapers and had a considerable success.[4]

Late Victorian England, of course, was the golden age of the literary fairy tale. Lewis Carroll's Alice books and George MacDonald's *The Princess and the Goblin* had appeared shortly before Ford was born, and they were followed by dozens of imitations. The line between adult and juvenile fiction was less strict then than it is now, and adult writers like Charles Dickens, William Thackeray, Oscar Wilde, and Christina Rossetti (who was Ford's aunt by marriage) all wrote fairy stories; Ford's project was therefore not unusual.

The plot of *The Brown Owl* follows the standard structural model of the fairy tale as outlined by Claude Bremond:[5]

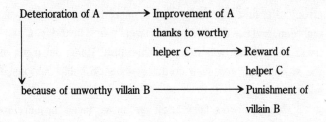

Its heroine, the Princess Ismara, suffers "deterioration" at the start of the story when her father, the king, dies, leaving in charge a chancellor who turns out to be an evil magician. The princess is protected from his various schemes by a large owl, the classic animal guardian, who also helps to unite her with a prince. The pattern is repeated in several episodes, as the magician is routed and returns again in different disguises and with different helpers.

The style of *The Brown Owl*, like that of many contemporary fairy tales, varies between flowery-elaborate and comic-realistic. Ford's descriptions tend to be conventionally pretty: "A beautiful day was dawning after the last night's rain, and the sun was rising brightly over the edge of the blue sea. . . . everything was quiet except the shrill chirp of a solitary sparrow."[6]

There is a good deal of rather heavy-handed farce involving the court doctor and his umbrella, a dwarf and a giant, and so on. *The Brown Owl* also contains the customary ironic asides and references to contemporary events for the amusement of the adult reader. For example, the wicked chancellor is said to be "inciting the people of far-off lands such as Mesopotamia and Ireland to rebel,"[7] and in his last and most dangerous transformation he is called "The Knight of London" and aided by a giant named Magog.[8]

Other aspects of the tale seem to be more personal to Ford, even prophetic. The Knight of London, who destroys all his opponents, can be defeated only by a paper sword and paper armor — the same weapons that Ford himself was to employ all his life. Princess Ismara is described as looking very much like Ford's sister, Juliet, who also had blue eyes and long, rippling golden hair; and she is extremely active, courageous, and enterprising for a Victorian heroine. She does not wait at home when the enemy attacks but leads her soldiers into battle; she is also so skilled in diplomacy that she wins most of her opponents over to her own side. Like latter-day feminists she refuses to be addressed as a child, declaring: "Now I won't be called a girl, for I'm nineteen, you know. His Majesty the Emperor of India there insulted me by calling me a girl, and I have not forgiven him yet."[9] Though his tone here is gently mocking, Ford appears to have admired independent, outspoken women. All the women he formed serious attachments to were strong-minded, and three were also self-supporting. Two of them, Stella Bowen and Janice Biala, were successful painters, and the third, Violet Hunt, a successful novelist.

It is also interesting to look at the story of *The Brown Owl* in terms of family history. Ford, Juliet, and their brother, Oliver, spent their earliest years in Hammersmith — then a separate, almost rural suburb of London. But early in 1889, when Ford was barely sixteen, his father, Dr. Hueffer, died and the family was separated. Mrs. Hueffer and the two boys went to live with her parents, Ford Madox Brown and his wife, near Regent's Park in London. Juliet, then only eight, was boarded two houses away with Mrs. Hueffer's sister Lucy Rossetti and her husband and four children.

The Brown Owl opens with the death of a beloved father, King Intafernes. The grieving heroine is protected by an old owl, which is brown — perhaps Ford Madox Brown.

At first it seems difficult and ill-tempered, like Ford and Juliet's grandfather. As Ford wrote later, Brown "had his irascibilities, his fits of passion when, tossing his white head, his mane of hair would fly all over his face, and when he would blaspheme impressively."[10] Yet after one got to know him he was not frightening; Ford spoke of him as "the finest man I ever knew,"[11] and Juliet remembered him as "one of the kindest, gentlest, handsomest old gentlemen that ever lived."[12]

In Ford's story the brown owl is also gradually revealed as a wise and noble being and finally as the spirit of the princess's dead father. It is as if, through his fairy tale, the young Ford is consciously or unconsciously urging his little sister to let their grandfather take the place of their lost father. Ford Madox Brown's enthusiasm for *The Brown Owl* may also have been partly due to his conscious or unconscious recognition of its hidden message. In the two illustrations he did for the book the princess looks very much like a grown-up Juliet, and the owl's eyes resemble his own spectacles.

Who, then, is the wicked chancellor who disguises himself as the Knight of London and tries and fails to take King Intafernes's place? Could he be a version of Ford's uncle William Rossetti, in whose house Juliet was living? Rossetti, the most practical and conventional member of a very Bohemian family, was Secretary of the Inland Revenue (the British tax office) and thus also a high government official in an economic post; it is possible that his cautious attitude toward money had displeased the already extravagant Ford.

After *The Brown Owl, The Feather,*[13] published a year later, comes as a considerable disappointment. It is rambling and disorganized; probably nobody who did not have to write a scholarly article would read it through (the pages of the Cornell copy had not been cut in more than eighty-six years). Again we have an independent-minded princess, a kingdom ruled by a wicked usurper, a giant, and a prince. The principal magic device is an eagle's feather that gives invisibility and makes it possible for the princess to go on a supernatural voyage to the moon, save the prince's life, and play many tiresome practical jokes on friends and enemies alike. The conventions of the fairy tale are violated by the inclusion of episodes involving the goddess Diana, the Three Fates, and the Man in the Moon.

There are some nice touches. Diana lives in the moon in a Greek temple made entirely of green cheese and is militantly chaste ("I hate men — nasty, vulgar things!" she remarks[14]). But there is also a lot of meaningless horseplay and many conversations full of bad puns that have the air of having been included only to pad out the story. The tone of the book is more cynical and sour than that of *The Brown Owl*. When the prince brings the princess home and is congratulated by the populace, Ford remarks, "This is a habit of populaces, they are all fond of congratulating anyone who is successful — but they never assist anyone to success if they can help it."[15]

Although *The Feather* is dedicated "To Juliet," the description of Princess Ernalie — who has brown hair and hazel eyes — sounds more like Elsie Martindale, the fifteen-year-old girl who was in two years to become Ford's wife. Possibly the dedication has a double meaning; Shakespeare's Juliet, like Elsie, was a very young girl. In the summer of 1892 Ford was already writing to her and calling on her regularly — and beginning to annoy her parents, who thought that Elsie was much too young to have a serious suitor. In the story, when Princess Ernalie tells her father of her feelings for the prince, the king exclaims, "You don't mean to say that you're in love with one another? Now I call that too bad."[16] But as befits a fairy tale his opposition is fleeting. The princess starts to cry, "and that of course softened the heart of her father. 'There,

there,' he said as if he were soothing a baby. 'Don't cry, you shall marry the Prince.' "[17]

In real life things did not go so smoothly for Ford and Elsie. By the summer of 1893 Dr. and Mrs. Martindale's annoyance at the romance had hardened into serious opposition. The Martindales were rich, respectable Victorian parents with no particular reverence for the arts. Though Ford had already published two books, they thought of him as "an irresponsible young man unlikely ever to earn a decent living" and "suspected him of wanting to marry Elsie for her money."[18] The more they saw of his influence over their daughter, the less they liked him; and in March of 1894 Dr. Martindale forbade him to come to the house again. Soon afterward he arranged to send Elsie away to the country, where, he hoped, Ford could not get at her.

On March 16, therefore, Elsie was put on a train to Winchelsea to visit an aunt. But she never arrived there; at a way station she eluded the older sister who was her chaperon, returned to London, and took another train to Bath, where Ford had arranged for her to stay with relatives sympathetic to his suit. Dr. Martindale responded by trying to get Elsie made a ward in Chancery in order to force her to return home. But before the law could act, on May 17, she and Ford were married; she was seventeen, and he twenty.

The Queen Who Flew, Ford's best book for children, was written during his courtship of Elsie Martindale and appeared in 1894, about a week before their wedding.[19] It is a first-rate story, lively, imaginative, and well written; stylistically it represents a great advance over the two earlier books. It compares favorably with contemporary fairy tales by such writers as Andrew Lang and Oscar Wilde and should be far better known today than it is.

Ford was aware of the romantic parallel between the story of *The Queen Who Flew* and his own; indeed, soon after he and Elsie had returned together to London he arranged with a journalist friend to place an article connecting fact and fairy tale in a daily newspaper, the *Star*. "A Poet's Love Affair. A Chancery Court Chapter of 'The Queen Who Flew' " appeared on June 6, 1894, and three other newspapers later picked up the story, creating considerable publicity for the book.[20]

The Queen Who Flew is not only an allegory of Ford's love affair with Elsie Martindale but in effect predicts its outcome. Young Queen Elrida, the heroine, is lonely, bored, and overprotected; her kingdom is in effect ruled by a sour, heavily bearded regent named Lord Blackjowl.* The queen's only companion is a talking bat who shows her a flower that gives the power of flight. She makes herself a wreath of the flowers and flies away over the castle wall, becoming involved in a series of adventures. At one point in the story another large, disagreeable, black-bearded man called King Mark (*Mar*-tindale?) tries to kill Queen Elrida because she has refused to marry him. He throws her off a tall tower, but she merely flies away, while he is imprisoned by his oppressed subjects and starves to death. This fantasy revenge on Dr. Martindale may appear rather extreme, but the situation before Elsie's elopement was extreme. At one point, for instance, Mrs. Martindale told her daughter that she would rather see her dead than married to Ford.

One interesting feature of *The Queen Who Flew* is its antiaristocratic, antimilitary bias, otherwise rare in Ford's work. The unpleasant Lord Blackjowl has strong reactionary opinions. When it is proposed that Queen Elrida give her worn-out stockings to the poor and she, having lived a very sheltered life, asks, "What are the poor?" Lord Blackjowl

*Dr. Martindale was a tall man with a full beard. In the photograph reproduced in Mizener's biography the beard is white, but his mustache remains dark; he may have been a Lord Blackjowl earlier in life.

replies, "The poor are wicked, idle people — too wicked to work and earn the money, and too dirty to wear stockings."[21] The queen, on the other hand, risks her life to get food for a beggar and is shocked by the wanton destructiveness of the soldiers.

The Queen Who Flew has an antiaristocratic and also antitraditional conclusion. This annoyed the reviewer for the *Academy,* who was otherwise well disposed toward the book; he remarked, "The story is well, but not too well written, and will probably please a large class of readers. The ending however . . . will, it is to be hoped, displease the lovers of old fairy lore."[22] Contrary to the traditions of "old fairy lore," the queen does not marry a king, nor is she restored to her own kingdom; instead she retires to the country. In the course of her adventures she has been taken in by a blind plowman and his mother. Acting on the advice of her friend the bat, she makes tea out of her wreath of magic flowers and gives it to the blind man, whose sight is thus restored. She appoints the bat as king in her place and goes off to marry the plowman and live happily ever after in his cottage.

Ford thus expresses the hope that Elsie will choose love in a cottage with him over London luxury and loneliness. He also echoes his recurring dream of a self-sufficient rural life as what he called a "Small Producer." This was not just a fantasy; Ford did spend much of his life in the country, though he was too restless to stay in one place for long. As he wrote much later: "I have dug, hoed, pruned, and sometimes even harvested twenty-six kitchen gardens that I can remember. . . . If I had not so constantly travelled, I should have reaped better harvests and written more and better books."[23]

Apart from its ending, *The Queen Who Flew,* unlike its predecessor, follows the traditional fairy story pattern. The central episode in which Queen Elrida flies over the countryside with the wild geese, who later turn out to be enchanted mortals, is very well done. Though it may have been inspired by such old folktales as "The Six Swans" (Grimm), it also looks ahead to one of the classics of children's literature, published thirteen years later, Selma Lagerlöf's *The Wonderful Adventures of Nils* (1906–7). It would be interesting to know whether Lagerlöf had read or heard of Ford's story, some passages of which recall her own account of Nils's flight with the wild geese over Sweden.

> And then, towards sunset, they all rose in the air, and the Queen with them, and went whirling round in great clouds of rustling pinions, dyed red in the sunset, geese and peewits, and snipe and herons, all wheeling about in sheer delight of life; until, when the sun was almost down, the geese, with a great cry of farewell, flew off through the gloaming with the Queen towards the hut.[24]

It will be noticed that Ford's first three children's books all feature heroines who fly with or by the agency of large birds, or, in the case of Elrida, a bat. Four of the nine stories in his fourth juvenile, *Christina's Fairy Book* (1906), also contain flying females, and in two of them fairies are carried over long distances by birds — in one case a gull, in the other a crow. It is impossible to say what this may have meant to Ford, though both Freudians and Jungians would certainly have suggestions. A recent study of Ford's work proposes that these flying creatures represent "a guiding or transforming element, . . . a spirituality, . . . a power within the psyche" and suggests that ultimately Ford's fairy tales are about the power of the feminine principle.[25]

The illustrations for Ford's first two books featured the owl and the eagle. Wild geese appear on every page of *The Queen Who Flew* as part of the elegant border design by C.R.B. Barnett, which is also reproduced on the cover of the trade edition. Ford Madox Brown was unable to illustrate this book; he had died in October 1893, after giving his blessing to his grandson's courtship of Elsie Martindale. But Brown's friend Edward Burne-Jones contributed a frontispiece, a red-crayon drawing of a girl in Pre-Raphaelite costume pouring water from a vase; though attractive and typical of his work, it bears no relation to the story.

After their wedding Ford and Elsie went to live in a country village in Kent, where Ford started the first of his many gardens. In spite of recurring worries about money they were happy during these early years. Ford was working steadily, and Elsie's parents gradually came to accept the marriage. In July 1897 their daughter Christina was born, and in April 1900 her sister, Katherine. Ford began to write the poems and tell the stories that were later to be collected in *Christina's Fairy Book.*[26]

This final children's book, though it has moments of wit and charm, is weaker and slighter than *The Brown Owl* or *The Queen Who Flew,* nor does it have the energy and invention of *The Feather.* In writing for his own daughters Ford was handicapped by a sentimental and fearful view of childhood. He saw Christina as very small and vulnerable, in need of constant protection, as he describes her in the dedicatory poem "To Christina at Nightfall," first published in 1901, when she was four:

> Little thing, ah, little mouse,
> Creeping through the twilit house,
>
> . . . .
>
> Good night! The fire is burning low;
> Put out the lamp;
> Lay down the weary little head
> Upon the small white bed.
> Up from the sea the night winds blow,

Across the hill, across the marsh;
  Chill and harsh, harsh and damp,
  The night winds blow.
But, while the slow hours go,
I, who must fall before you, late shall wait
  and keep
    Watch and ward,
    Vigil and guard,
    Where you sleep.[27]

As a boy Ford had been frightened by the stories of his nurse, who had a predilection for tales of violence and disaster; he was determined to shelter his daughters from the sort of night terrors he had known. In the prefatory note to *Christina's Fairy Book* he writes: "As a child I used to see wolves and demons: I can feel still some of the agonies I felt then. I wished to spare my children some of these fears by peopling their shadows with little friendly beings."[28] Unfortunately, this wish led him to produce shallow and whimsical brief tales of a type all too common at the time, in which the fairies are tiny, silly, helpless creatures who wear cowslip caps and whisper in seashells. Ford's fairies are so small that one gets caught in the fur of the family dog, Cromwell, when he is out for a walk and is expelled with flea powder. Only then is he noticed:

When I came in in the evening, after you had gone to bed [Ford writes] I heard a little clitter-clittering noise against the pictures, as if it were a moth beating against the glasses; and then I saw a fairy, not so large as a moth, in blue scale armour and with blue wings all dusted with insect powder. . . . this fairy was quite blinded with what Mother had sprinkled into Cromwell's fur, and there it was, battering against everything in the room, trying to find a way out.[29]

Six of the nine stories in *Christina's Fairy Book* are of this sort. Two others, "Mary and Matty and Lob" and "Bingel and Bengel," are conventionally told tales of the well-known "Kind and Unkind" type, in which a good child who helps a brownie or dwarf is rewarded and a bad one mildly punished. Internal evidence suggests that the stories were made up over a period of some years. In the early ones, only Christina is addressed; in "The Fairy Who Lived in a Steeple," we hear that the poor child who has been given a two-shilling piece can now buy "some almonds and some raisins and some chocolates and some figs, and some cotton to sew up the hole in her pocket, and a beautiful doll for her baby sister,"[30] suggesting that it must have been written in 1902 or later, when Christina would have been old enough to sew and Katherine old enough to appreciate a doll, though still a baby.

The seven poems that appear between the tales are a mixed lot. Most are slight and conventional, weak imitations of Robert Louis Stevenson or of old nursery rhymes. But "The Unwritten Song" has real Edwardian charm, as it proposes

A song of greeny glow-worm lights,
In the long grass of summer nights,
Or flitting showers of firefly flights,
   Where summer woods hang deep:

Of wavering, noiseless owls that find
Their way by dusk, and of a kind
And drowsy, drowsy ocean wind
   That lulls the sea to sleep.[31]

This was the period of Ford's close association with the novelist Joseph Conrad, with whom he collaborated on *The Inheritors* (1901) and *Romance* (1903). The Ford (then Hueffer) and Conrad families were often together, sometimes sharing a house. Christina and Katherine played with Conrad's son Borys. "The Three Friends," which appears in *Christina's Fairy Book,* has a verse for each of the children. "Pumpums" was their nickname for Ford, "Mummums" is Elsie, and "Blank-dash" is Conrad:*

There was an old Pumpums who said,
"It is time little kids were in bed,"
  So they took up Christina
  And washed her much cleaner,
And carried her quickly to bed.

There was an old Mummums who said,
"It is time little girls were in bed,"
  So they caught up Miss Katherine
  And made a great lather in
Her bath and then popped her in bed.

There was an old Blank-dash who said,
"It is time little scamps were in bed,"
  So they bore Master Borys
  Upstairs where the door is,
And bathed him and put him to bed,
  And they said
"Oh it's peaceful now they are in bed!"³²

The years just before the publication of *Christina's Fairy Book* were difficult ones. Elsie was often ill; there was never enough money, and Ford had completed two books for which he could not find a publisher.³³ Gradually he fell into a state of severe depression complicated by bouts of anxiety and agoraphobia. His state of mind is reflected in the last story of *Christina's Fairy Book,* which begins, "There was once an old pumpums who was tired and ill and sick and sorry. And

---

*Pumpums, Mummums, and Blank-dash were "old" only by courtesy; at the time this verse was composed Ford was probably about twenty-nine, Elsie twenty-six, and Conrad forty-five.

he lay on the big bed beside his little kiddies; and his little kiddies said: 'Tell us a tale, Pumpums.' "[34] Ford then becomes the bough of a tree outside the window and proceeds to tell a tale involving the theft of a king's jewels by a magpie, a false accusation against the page the princess loves, and a trial and a hanging that is only saved from being fatal when the bough breaks, revealing the true culprit and uniting the princess and the page. Ford seems to be saying that justice can be done and happiness achieved only if he himself is destroyed. The meaning he suggests in the text is vaguer but no less sad: "So the tired Pumpums told them the story. And when he had finished telling it, he added: 'I suppose that the moral is that there is no avoiding troubles, even if one turns into tree boughs. All the same, I hope my little kiddies will find, somewhere in the world, the good place where no troubles are. Who knows?' "[35]

Arthur Mizener has suggested that much of Ford's depression and anxiety at this period "was neurotic, a product of the destructive clash between his dreams of glory and the actualities of his existence."[36] Better times were soon to come for Ford, but he was to suffer all his life from this clash between fantasy and reality. At times his romantic daydreams of past and present success became so real to him that he repeated them to others, with disastrous results when the real truth became known. As Ezra Pound put it: "He was the helpless victim of his own imagination. . . . He could not extricate himself from what he imagined and what actually happened. . . . He told stories about himself constantly and as the stories were retold he embroidered them. . . . He fabricated and elaborated his life as assiduously as he fabricated and elaborated his books."[37]

Ford was aware of this weakness in himself, but he could not control it; he preferred fantasy to fact. He knew, too, that most of the world did not share this preference.

For children, however, the world of the imagination was as real as it was for him. While his daughters were young they could share this world; but all too soon they outgrew it. So at the end of *Christina's Fairy Book,* Ford writes, with a pathos not entirely destroyed by self-pity,

> I think that this is the last fairy tale that this Pumpums will tell his kiddies. For now when at nightfall he goes to them they say no longer: "Tell us a fairy tale," but: "Tell us some history." For, you see, they have grown out of believing in the untruths that are most real of all, and they are beginning to believe in these truths that are so false. And I do not know that that does not make this Pumpums a little sad. Still, it is the way of all flesh.[38]

8

Animal Liberation

BEATRIX POTTER

Nearly ninety years ago, in London, a woman escaped from prison with the help of a rabbit. It was not a modern prison, with facilities for education and recreation and a chance of parole, but a tall, dark, stuffy Victorian house; and the prisoner, who had been confined there for most of her thirty-six years, was under sentence for life. The rabbit's name, of course, was Peter.

If Beatrix Potter had been born in this century, or if she had been born a man, there is little doubt that she would have become a famous painter, a well-known naturalist, or both. It was her misfortune to be the only daughter of rich, pretentious, unimaginative, ultraconservative parents whose view of what was proper for a well-bred girl ruled out almost every human interest and activity. Beatrix was never allowed to go to school, where she might have picked up unsuitable ideas and rude habits; and she never had any friends of her own age — her only companion was her brother, Bertram, six years younger.

Beatrix and Bertram lived an isolated life with their strict Scottish nurse and a succession of governesses on the top floor of their expensive, depressing South Kensington house, at an extreme emotional as well as physical distance from their parents. Their father and mother almost never went up to the nursery to see the children and only occasionally asked to have them brought down into the parlor for inspection. Mr. Potter, following the life of a gentleman, spent his days at his club; Mrs. Potter occupied herself in directing the staff of servants and making formal calls.

What seems to have saved Beatrix and her brother from complete stultification was the family holidays in Scotland and in England's Lake District. There their parents' lack of interest in them had advantages. While Mr. and Mrs. Potter reproduced in boring detail the rigid pattern of their London lives — the elaborate, silent meals, the carriage drive at two P.M., et cetera — the children could explore the surrounding gardens and woods and fields and streams, the village lanes and farmyards, without interference. Beatrix helped find eggs in the barn; she fed the poultry and made friends with the farm dogs and cows and pigs.

Everything about the countryside fascinated the Potter children. They collected plants, birds' eggs, and insects; they made pets of mice, rabbits, an owl, and a hedgehog. Both Beatrix and Bertram were naturally gifted artists, and they filled sketchbooks with drawings of whatever they saw. Beatrix's watercolors of caterpillars and flowers, made at the age of eight and nine, look like the work of someone much older and show the same charm, delicacy, and accuracy of observation that were to characterize her published books. She also had a gift for fantasy and soon began making up stories set in the local landscape. "I do not remember a time when I did not try to invent pictures," she wrote later, "and make for myself a fairyland amongst the wild flowers, the animals, fungi, mosses, woods and streams, all the thousand objects of the countryside."[1]

As the children grew up, Beatrix became even more isolated. "Her parents seem not to have noticed that she was unnaturally lonely. Her brother Bertram . . . disappeared to school, and she had no other friends. She knew no neighborhood children, and was given no opportunity of knowing any."[2]

Bertram, after leaving school, became a painter who specialized in Scottish mists and crags. There was no question of a career for his sister, who remained confined to the house. At seventeen she was allowed to take twelve lessons in painting, but no more; her parents decided that they cost too much. Later, her greatest regret was that she had never studied anatomy or learned to draw from the human figure — in her youth thought extremely improper for a young lady. Her knowledge of animal anatomy, as evidenced in her illustrations, was scientific and exact, based on study from life. Already as a child she had dissected dead mice, birds, and even a fox, and boiled and reassembled their skeletons.

Beatrix Potter was now of an age at which most proper Victorian girls were married off, and her parents apparently made some efforts in this direction. But Beatrix, who had grown into a plain, painfully shy young woman, had no interest in London society. When she was sent to a fashionable party she sat in a corner, refusing to dance or be introduced to anyone, and left as early as possible. She preferred to go to art exhibitions, and to the nearby Natural History Museum, where she spent long hours copying insects, fossils, and stuffed animals.

"I can't settle to anything but my painting,"[3] she wrote in her journal, and again, "I cannot rest, I must draw, however poor the result, and when I have a bad time come over me it is a stronger desire than ever."[4] She retained her fascination with the smallest and most humble details of the natural world: how the entrance of a rabbit hole looks, the way feathers grow on a wing or bark around a knothole in an old oak.

Along with her art, Beatrix Potter continued her interest in botany, especially during her holidays. She rejoiced in the discovery and painting of new species of mushrooms and developed an original theory about the propagation of lichens, which she believed were composed of fungi living in association with algae. (As it turned out, she was quite right about this.) For years she was unable to get the male scientific community even to look at her discoveries.

Finally, in 1896, her uncle Sir Henry Roscoe, a well-known chemist, offered his help. He took her to Kew Gardens so that she could show her beautiful and accurate drawings of mushrooms to the authorities there; he also encouraged his niece to write a paper on her theories, which he arranged to have read before the Linnaean Society. Beatrix could not read it herself, because women were not allowed at the society's meetings. Yet his efforts were in vain. The botanists at Kew sneered at Beatrix's drawings as amateurish (although many years later they were used to illustrate a textbook on British mushrooms), and no notice whatsoever was taken of her paper.

Beatrix Potter was now over thirty: still shy and awkward in company, plain, dowdily dressed, unmarried and by the standards of her parents' world unlikely ever to be married, with nothing to look forward to but years of serving as an unpaid companion to her conventional and exacting mother. It is not surprising to learn that during this period of her life she was often ill, suffering from faintness, rheumatic pains, and recurring depression and fatigue.

But she did not abandon her art. Having failed to make her mark in the adult world, she turned, like many gifted women before her, to children. At first it was mainly to console herself that she began drawing pictures of mice and rabbits, and sending illustrated story-letters to the children she knew. However, by 1900 the private success of her tales led her to think of trying to get them published commercially. *The Tale of Peter Rabbit* was sent to, and rejected by, six publishers, but she did not give up; instead she herself paid to have 250 copies printed. They sold almost instantly, and two years later the book was accepted by Frederick Warne & Company — one of the best commercial decisions that firm ever made.

When it first appeared, *Peter Rabbit* was something completely new in children's literature. For one thing, it was child-sized. Beatrix Potter was determined that her books should be made to fit children's hands and not to impress adults. The oversized and overpriced picture books of that time — like those of our own — were often so expensive that most families could not afford them and so heavy that a four- or five-year-old could manage them only by squatting on the floor. But *Peter Rabbit* cost only a shilling, and it could be tucked into a pocket and taken along on trips, to school, and even to bed.

Moreover, Beatrix Potter refused to talk down to children. Believing that they wanted and needed to learn new things, she deliberately included at least one difficult word in each of her books. And her illustrations, unlike so many then and now, were not simplified and cheapened for children. Beatrix Potter brought all her skill as an artist to these pictures. Peter Rabbit and the rest are not cute caricatures but were drawn from life, and so were all the details of their surroundings.

One special attraction of these books was that Beatrix Potter portrayed the world from a mouse's- or rabbit's- or small child's–eye view. The vantage point in her exquisite watercolors varies from a few inches to a few feet from the ground, like that of a toddler. Indeed, when I first came across the Peter Rabbit books, I had no idea that Beatrix Potter was a grown-up woman: I thought of her as a little girl.

Certainly she was small enough to look at hollyhocks and tables and big dogs from below and to see everything in close-up. In her illustrations a cabbage leaf, the pattern of moss on a stump, a painted china cup, or a spool of red thread are seen with the short-range clarity of focus that is physiologically possible for most of us only in early childhood.

Another new and very important feature of Beatrix Potter's books was that they broke completely with the traditional pattern of the animal tale or fable, which had always been used to point an improving moral. Usually the unconventional message is concealed behind a screen of conventional morality, which might have fooled adults, but not their juniors and betters. In *Peter Rabbit,* for instance, Potter at first seems to be recommending restraint and obedience. At the end, Peter is sent to bed in disgrace after his exciting adventures in Mr. McGregor's garden, while good little Flopsy, Mopsy, and Cottontail "had bread and milk and blackberries for supper."[5] But when I asked a class of students which character in the book they would have preferred to be, they voted unanimously for Peter, recognizing the concealed moral of the story: that disobedience and exploration are more fun than good behavior, and not really all that dangerous, whatever Mother may say.

Consciously or not, children know that the author's sympathy and interest are with Peter, and with Tom Kitten and the Two Bad Mice; with impertinent, reckless Squirrel Nutkin, and not with the other timid, good squirrels or with obedient, dull little Flopsy, Mopsy, and Cottontail. One further proof of this is that although Peter loses his jacket and shoes in Mr. McGregor's garden, a few books later he is back again looking for lettuce with his cousin Benjamin Bunny, quite unrepentant.

Evidently, there is something attractive to children about animals, especially the sort we meet most often in

Beatrix Potter: rabbits, mice, kittens, and squirrels. For nearly ninety years young children have loved her books; they seem to feel comfortable with her characters, even akin to them somehow. And after all, it is not so long since they too were inarticulate, instinctive small creatures, with simple animal needs and pleasures. They still know what it feels like to steal food when larger people's backs are turned, as Peter Rabbit does, or to playfully disorder an older child's dollhouse, like the Two Bad Mice.

Peter Rabbit and the twenty-three books that followed it brought Beatrix Potter more than money and fame; in 1905 her editor, Norman Warne, fell in love with her and asked her to marry him. Mr. and Mrs. Potter were shocked and furious; Warne was not a gentleman, he was "in trade," and they refused to give their consent. But Beatrix Potter was now an independent woman, and she announced her engagement. She also wrote and illustrated one of her most delightful books, *The Tale of Two Bad Mice* (1904). Norman Warne helped her by buying the dolls and photographing the dollhouse that he had built for his niece.

As Suzanne Rahn has pointed out in an interesting article, this story is the only one of Beatrix Potter's in which a married couple appears. In it Tom Thumb and Hunca Munca, who were named after Beatrix's own pet mice, invade a large and pretentious dollhouse. Angry because the fancy food turns out to be made of painted plaster, they first vandalize the house and then carry off part of its contents. Ms. Rahn suggests that the dollhouse, with its useless luxuries and stiff, helpless inhabitants, represents the Potter residence in South Kensington and that the two lively and destructive intruders — who at the end make partial restitution — are Beatrix and Norman Warne.[6]

The Tale of Two Bad Mice predicts a happy future and many children for Tom Thumb and Hunca Munca. Yet before

Beatrix Potter and Norman Warne could be married, he became seriously ill; he was discovered to have leukemia, and died the summer of 1905. Unhappy as she was, the experience of defying her family had given Beatrix Potter strength; she went on writing and publishing, and she used her royalties to buy a farm in the Lake District. At first she could visit it only for a week or two at a time because of her parents' demands. Gradually, though, she began to spend more time there and to buy more property.

In 1913 she became engaged to a local lawyer, William Heelis, married him in spite of her parents' objections, and moved to Hill Top Farm for good. This triumph is celebrated, several critics have suggested, in *The Tale of Pigling Bland,* published in the month of her wedding, October 1913. The book is illustrated with a view of her garden at Hill Top Farm and ends with the escape of Pigling Bland and a "perfectly lovely little black Berkshire pig,"[7] Pig-wig, from a claustrophobic kitchen to Beatrix Potter's beloved Lake District.

> The sun rose while they were crossing the moor, a dazzle of light over the tops of the hills. The sunshine crept down the slopes into the peaceful green valleys, where little white cottages nestled in gardens and orchards.
>
> "That's Westmorland," said Pig-wig. She dropped Pigling's hand and commenced to dance.[8]

In *The Tale of Little Pig Robinson* (1930), the protagonist goes even further, settling on a desert island and becoming the pig "with a ring at the end of his nose"[9] who was so useful to Edward Lear's Owl and Pussycat.

In her last thirty years Beatrix Potter published only four more books. She devoted herself instead to farming, sheep raising, gardening, and the preservation of the countryside. Even then the Lake District was in danger of becoming a clutter of tourist camps, roadside stands, and cheap developments. Beatrix Potter worked to bring as much land as possible under the ownership of the National Trust, which looks after parks and historic places in Britain; and in her will she left the Trust most of her own property. Today you can visit Hill Top Farm and the nearby village of Sawrey and find them almost exactly as they were in the days of Peter Rabbit, Squirrel Nutkin, and Mrs. Tiggy-winkle the hedgehog; you can walk through the surrounding country and see their wild descendants enjoying the world that Beatrix Potter loved and recorded and saved for them.

9

Modern Magic

E. NESBIT

Victorian literary fairy tales tend to have a conservative moral and political bias. Under their charm and invention is usually an improving lesson: adults know best; good, obedient, patient, and self-effacing little boys and girls are rewarded by the fairies, and naughty assertive ones are punished. In the most widely read British authors of the period — Frances Browne, Mrs. Craik, Mrs. Ewing, Mrs. Molesworth, and even the greatest of them all, George MacDonald — the usual manner is that of a kind lady or gentleman delivering a delightfully disguised sermon. Only Lewis Carroll's Alice books completely avoid this didactic tone. The strange creatures Alice meets are not her moral or intellectual superiors, and she does not become a more model child as a result of her adventures. But though Carroll's dreamlike plots, brilliantly grotesque comic characters, and verbal wit were soon widely imitated by others, these writers usually could not resist adding or implying a moral.

In the final years of Victoria's reign, however, an author appeared who was to challenge this pattern so energetically and with such success that it is possible now to speak of juvenile literature as before and after E. Nesbit. Though there are foreshadowings of her characteristic manner in Charles

Dickens's "Holiday Romance" and Kenneth Grahame's *The Golden Age*, Nesbit was the first to write at length for children as intellectual equals and in their own language. Her books were startlingly innovative in other ways: they took place in contemporary England and recommended socialist solutions to its problems; they presented a modern view of childhood; and they used magic both as a comic device and as a serious metaphor for the power of the imagination. Every writer of children's fantasy since Nesbit's time is indebted to her — and so are some authors of adult fiction.

The woman who overturned so many conventions of children's literature was herself a scandalously unconventional member of the Victorian upper middle class, into which she was born in 1858. As a child, Edith Nesbit was a rebellious, hot-tempered tomboy, and no doubt a trial to her gentle widowed mother. She hated most of the schools she was sent to and declared later that she had "never been able to love a doll."[1] Her passions were reading, riding, swimming, and playing pirates with her older brothers during holidays. She also, however, had nightmares and suffered from imaginative fear of the dark and of death.*

In 1880, at twenty-one, Edith Nesbit married a handsome young businessman named Hubert Bland; she was seven months pregnant at the time. Shortly after the wedding, disaster struck: Bland became seriously ill with smallpox, and his partner disappeared with all the capital of the firm. Somehow, Edith had to support herself, her baby, and her convalescent husband. She did it by painting greeting cards, giving recitations, and turning out a flood of ephemeral verses,

*Julia Briggs, *A Woman of Passion*, p. 12. Ms. Briggs most perceptively remarks that in *The Bastable Children* Nesbit "presents herself as twins — the morally courageous and determined Alice and her vulnerable brother Noel, subject to fits of poetry, fainting and tears" (Briggs, p. xvii).

stories, essays, and novels. After he recovered, Hubert Bland also took up the pen, eventually becoming a well-known political journalist; yet during the thirty-four years of her marriage Edith, and not her husband, was the economic mainstay of their large family. Both the Blands were lifelong socialists, founders and prominent members of the Fabian Society. At one time or another, E. Nesbit supported most of the radical causes of her day — and many of its radical fads, including dress reform, psychic research, and the claim that Francis Bacon wrote the plays of Shakespeare.

The work E. Nesbit produced between the ages of twenty and forty gives almost no sign of what was to come: it is conventional and often, to the modern taste, sentimental. Then suddenly, in 1898, the Bastable stories began to appear. The first volume, *The Story of the Treasure Seekers,* which related the lively, comic adventures of six London children who try to restore the family fortunes, was instantly popular. What seems to have released E. Nesbit's genius was the decision to tell the story through — in a sense, to become — Oswald Bastable, a child much after her own pattern: bold, quick-tempered, egotistic, and literary.

The success of *The Treasure Seekers* made it possible for the Blands to leave London and move to Weld Hall in Kent, a large, beautiful eighteenth-century brick house that was to be E. Nesbit's home until almost the end of her life; it became the Moat House of the later Bastable stories. Over the next ten years she produced the books for which she is known today, books full of wit, energy, and invention.

Throughout their life together the Blands kept open house for what Nesbit's biographer, Doris Langley Moore, calls "a strange assortment of artists, writers, and politicians,"[2] plus an equally odd lot of poor relations, abandoned and illegitimate children, penniless would-be authors and artists, and cranks. H. G. Wells described their house in Kent as "a place to which one rushed down from town at the week-end to snatch one's bed before anyone else got it."³ Though most of their guests did not know this, the Blands' marriage as well as their house was what today would be called open, especially at the husband's end. Hubert Bland was constantly unfaithful; his wife, though hurt by his love affairs, usually ended by taking a sympathetic interest in the women involved. She also passed off two of his illegitimate children as her own and raised them along with her three.

As time went on, E. Nesbit also now and then formed romantic attachments — though the most famous of these, to George Bernard Shaw, never went beyond enthusiastic friendship. Even in late middle age she was the sort of woman men fall in love with: tall, good-looking, impulsive, charming, and completely unpredictable. Part of her charm was that in some sense she had never quite grown up. As her biographer reports, she "had all the caprices, the little petulances, the sulks, the jealousies, the intolerances, the selfishnesses of a child; and with them went a child's freshness of vision, hunger for adventure, remorse for unkindness, quick sensibility, and reckless generosity."⁴ Her appearance was untidy and strikingly Bohemian: she wore loose, trailing "aesthetic" dress (and sometimes, for bicycling, pantaloons); her arms were loaded with silver bangles and her abundant dark hair was bobbed; and in an era when only "fast women" smoked, she was never without tobacco and cigarette papers — a defiance of convention that may have been responsible for her recurrent bronchial troubles and eventually for her death.

PERHAPS it was because E. Nesbit remained emotionally about twelve years old all her life that she found it natural to speak as one intelligent child to another, in a tone now so common in juvenile fiction that it is hard to realize how radical and even shocking it would have seemed at the time. When she began her career the customary style of children's fiction was formal, leisurely, and gently didactic. Here, for instance, is a passage from George MacDonald's last great book, *The Princess and Curdie* (1882):

> The eyes of fathers and mothers are quick to read their children's looks, and when Curdie entered the cottage, his parents saw at once that something unusual had taken place. . . . There was a change upon Curdie, and father and mother felt there must be something to account for it, and therefore were pretty sure he had something to tell them. For when a child's heart is all right, it is not likely he will want to keep anything from his parents.[5]

And here is E. Nesbit's first classic work, *The Treasure Seekers:* "Of course as soon as we had promised to consult my father about business matters, we all gave up wanting to go into business. I don't know how it is, but having to consult about a thing with grown up people, even the bravest and the best, seems to make the thing not worth doing afterwards."[6]

When Nesbit writes in her own voice her tone is much the same: informal, direct, that of a sensible child coolly commenting on the world.

> People in books never can eat when they are in trouble, but I have noticed myself that if the trouble has gone on for some hours, eating is really rather a comfort. You don't enjoy it so much as usual, perhaps, but at any rate it is something to do, and takes the edge off your sorrow for a short time.[7]

> It is a curious thing that people only ask if you are enjoying yourself when you aren't.[8]

Even today her wholehearted adoption of the child's point of view sometimes surprises. In "The Cockatoucan," for instance, Nesbit explains why Matilda doesn't want to visit her great-aunt Willoughby:

> She would be asked about her lessons, and how many marks she had, and whether she had been a good girl. I can't think why grown-up people don't see how impertinent these questions are. Suppose you were to answer, "I'm top of my class, Auntie, thank you, and I'm very good. And now let's have a little talk about you. Aunt, dear, how much money have you got, and have you been scolding the servants again, or have you tried to be good and patient as a properly brought up aunt should be, eh, dear?"[9]

Not only is Nesbit's tone direct, humorous, and fast-moving; her children are modern and believable. They are not types seen by an adult, but individuals observed by their peers, each with his or her faults and virtues and passions. Though she tries to be fair and give everyone an equal chance at adventures and magic, she clearly prefers boys and girls of her own sort. In her stories, the sort of serious, diffident, well-behaved children who would have been the heroes and heroines of a typical Victorian fairy tale are portrayed as timid and dull — though a few of them can, with proper encouragement from their peers, improve.

The Treasure Seekers and its sequels are firmly rooted in the contemporary world. The Bastable children need to restore the family fortunes because their father's business partner has taken advantage of his illness to abscond with the firm's total assets, just as Hubert Bland's partner once did. The children's attempts to earn money by selling patent medicine, starting a newspaper, rescuing an old gentleman from danger (their own pet dog), or marrying a princess tend to produce comic disaster. In the sequels the Bastables' intended good deeds have a similar effect. By proper Victorian standards they behave badly — disobeying their elders, digging up gardens, trespassing, and playing practical jokes — but though they may be scolded and punished, they are always forgiven.

One especially radical, and at the time highly subversive, feature of Nesbit's tales is her implicit feminism. Her books are full of girls who are as brave and adventurous as their brothers; and even in her more conventional short fairy tales, the heroines never sit around waiting to be rescued. In "The Last of the Dragons," the princess remarks: "Father, darling, couldn't we tie up one of the silly little princes for the dragon to look at — and then I could go and kill the dragon . . . ? I fence much better than any of the princes we know."[10] Nesbit also occasionally strikes a blow for what is now called male liberation: this same princess falls in love with "a pale prince with large eyes and a head full of mathematics and philosophy"[11] who has completely neglected his fencing lessons.

In the Victorian fairy tale class lines tend to be sharply drawn and the superiority of the upper-class child taken for granted. Carroll's Alice is glad that she doesn't have to live in a poky little house like Mabel; and in Charles Kingsley's *The Water Babies,* Tom the chimney sweep has to forgive his cruel master Grimes and be washed as white as snow before he is a fit companion for the good little rich girl Miss Ellie.*

The main characters in Nesbit's books are usually middle-class, but some of her most sympathetic heroes and heroines, such as Mabel in *The Enchanted Castle,* represent a lower

---

*George MacDonald, however, is an exception to this rule. Curdie, the hero of *The Princess and the Goblin,* is the son of a miner, and Diamond in *At the Back of the North Wind* the son of a cabman.

stratum of society. Dickie, the hero of *Harding's Luck,* is almost uneducated and comes from the worst slums of East London, yet he is not only intelligent, imaginative, and courageous, but capable of self-sacrifice; while Edred, the future Lord Arden, is — at least at the start of the story — cowardly, mean, and rather stupid. His eventual reformation is not achieved with the help of surrogate parent figures, but through experience and the example of his peers.*

In the short fairy tale "The Mixed Mine," E. Nesbit reverses the standard Victorian plot in which a poor child is befriended and reformed by a more privileged one. Here it is the shabby Gustus who shows Edward how to get the best out of a magic telescope that enlarges whatever you look at through it; and it is Gustus who jollies Edward out of his fear of the consequences, remarking finally that his friend is "more like a man and less like a snivelling white rabbit now than what you was when I met you."[12] The implicit Fabian moral seems to be that intelligent artisans can show a scientifically illiterate and nervous middle class how to use the new technology to increase natural resources for the good of the whole society. (At the end of the story Gustus and Edward share a treasure and an Oxford education, and plan to start a school for slum kids.)

Though her working-class heroes and heroines are full of life and enterprise, Nesbit often portrays the extremely well born as stupid and dreary. In *The Treasure Seekers* Noel gets his wish and meets a real princess, but she turns out to be a dull, overdressed little girl who is afraid to play in the park. Most of Nesbit's fairy tale kings and queens are comic bunglers, and her court officials tend to be two-faced frauds with an up-to-date command of smarmy political rhetoric.

---

*Nesbit here anticipates by two years one of the central themes of Frances Hodgson Burnett's *The Secret Garden.*

When Uncle James, in the story of the same name, hears that a dragon has eaten his country's entire army, he sees an opportunity to get rid of his niece the princess and take control of the kingdom. He speaks to the populace as follows:

> "Friends — fellow citizens — I cannot disguise from myself or from you that this purple dragon is a poor penniless exile, a helpless alien in our midst. . . . The defenses of our country have been swallowed up," said Uncle James.
>
> Everyone thought of the poor army. . . .
>
> "Could we ever forgive ourselves if by neglecting a simple precaution we lost . . . our navy, our police, and our fire brigade? For I warn you that the purple dragon will respect nothing, however sacred."
>
> Everyone thought of themselves — and they said, "What is the simple precaution?" . . .
>
> "The present the dragon expects," said Uncle James cheerfully, "is a rather expensive one. But, when we give, it should not be in a grudging spirit, especially to visitors. What the dragon wants is a Princess. We have only one Princess, it is true, but far be it from us to display a miserly temper at such a moment."[13]

Nesbit's stories also take account of contemporary economic realities. Her families tend to be in financial trouble, just as the Blands so often were. Father is ill, or has lost his job or been defrauded by a business partner; he may even, as in *The Railway Children,* be in prison. Mother too may be ill (in *Five of Us, and Madeline* she has had a nervous breakdown), or she may be away caring for a sick relative. Often, as a result of these domestic disasters, the children have to go and stay with unsympathetic strangers in bleak, unattractive lodgings. Even when the family is intact it is usually in cramped economic circumstances. The situation is most depressing when they live in town: for, as Nesbit remarks in *Five Children and It,* "London is like a prison for children, especially if their relatives are not rich."[14]

In Nesbit's stories, even classic fairy tale characters may have to cope with Edwardian London. After the king and queen in "Princess and Hedge-Pig" are turned out of their castle by a usurper, their daughter finds them "living in quite a poor way in a semi-detached villa at Tooting" where "the garden is small and quite full of wet washing hung on lines" and the road "full of dust and perambulators."[15]

From the Fabian point of view, the Edwardian age was a period of material luxury and political smugness, combined with disregard for the environment. In Nesbit's fiction, urbanization is always associated with capitalist greed. The king in "Fortunatus Rex & Co." establishes "the largest speculative builders in the world":

> They bought up all the pretty woods and fields they could get and cut them up into squares, and grubbed up the trees and the grass and put streets there and lamp-posts and ugly little yellow brick houses, in the hopes that people would want to live in them. And curiously enough people did. So the King and his Co. made quite a lot of money.
>
> It is curious that nearly all the great fortunes are made by turning beautiful things into ugly ones. Making beauty out of ugliness is very ill-paid work.[16]

One of Nesbit's recurrent themes is the aesthetic unpleasantness not only of jerry-built modern suburbs but of cities in general and especially of London, that "hateful, dark, ugly place."[17] Many of us are now so accustomed to the nostalgic, prettified BBC version of Edwardian London that we have forgotten, if we ever knew, that in the early years of this century much of the city was filthy and many of its inhabitants sick or starving; the streets were fouled with horse manure and urine, the Thames polluted, and the air often unfit to breathe. (The pea-soup fogs that lend mystery and charm to the adventures of Sherlock Holmes were in fact a damp, poisonous smog.)

In *The Story of the Amulet* a rash wish brings the queen of Babylon, whom the children have met in the past, to London. She adores the Tower and the Thames but is appalled by the condition of the inhabitants.

> "But how badly you keep your slaves. How wretched and poor and neglected they seem," she said, as the cab rattled along the Mile End Road.
>
> "They aren't slaves; they're working-people," said Jane.
>
> "Of course they're working. That's what slaves are. Don't you tell me. Do you suppose I don't know a slave's face when I see it? Why don't their masters see that they're better fed and better clothed? . . . You'll have a revolt of your slaves if you're not careful," said the Queen.
>
> "Oh, no," said Cyril; "you see they have votes — that makes them safe not to revolt. It makes all the difference. Father told me so."
>
> "What is this vote?" asked the Queen. "Is it a charm? What do they do with it?"
>
> "I don't know," said the harassed Cyril; "it's just a vote, that's all! They don't do anything particular with it."
>
> "I see," said the Queen; "a sort of plaything."[18]

Later in the same book the amulet takes the children into a future in which England has become a Fabian Utopia, a city of parks and flowers with clean air and an unpolluted Thames. People live in beautiful, uncluttered houses and wear loose woolly clothes of the sort favored by William Morris and the Aesthetic Movement. There are no idle rich: everyone works and no one goes hungry; the schools are progressive and coeducational; and both men and women care for babies.

THE TYPICAL Victorian fantasy for children, though it may begin in the real world, soon moves into some timeless Wonderland or country at the back of the North Wind. One of Nesbit's most brilliant innovations was to reverse the process and bring magic into modern London. (In this, it has been pointed out, she may have been following the lead of a contemporary writer of adult fantasy, F. Anstey.) She was the first to imagine, for a child audience, what would be the actual consequences of the delivery by magic carpet of 199 Persian cats to the basement dining room of a house in Camden Town, or of the transformation of one's brother into a ten-foot boy giant.

Even Nesbit's short tales, though they may contain magicians and dragons and kings and queens, clearly take place in the present. The details of the stories, and the language in which they are told, are always up-to-date. Discarding the romantic diction of the fairy tale and its conventional epithets — the golden hair and milk-white steeds — she uses contemporary juvenile slang and draws her comparisons from the Edwardian child's world of experience. The dragon in "Uncle James" has "wings like old purple umbrellas that have been very much rained on,"[19] and the court officials in "The Book of Beasts" wear "gold coronets with velvet sticking up out of the middle like the cream in the very expensive jam tarts."[20] The hands of the unpleasant Miss Minto in *Five of Us, and Madeline* are "like hot goldfishes, red and wet."[21]

THOUGH WE tend to take it for granted, the importance of magic in juvenile literature needs some explanation. Why, in a world that is so wonderful and various and new to them, should children want to read about additional, unreal wonders? The usual explanation is a psychological one: magic provides an escape from reality or expresses fears and wishes. In the classic folktale, according to this theory, fear of starvation becomes a witch or a wolf, cannibalism an ogre. Desire shapes itself as a pot that is always full of porridge, a stick that will beat one's enemies on command, a mother who comes back to life as a benevolent animal or bird. Magic in children's literature, too, can make psychological needs and fears concrete; children confront and defeat threatening adults in the form of giants, or they become supernaturally large and strong; and though they cannot yet drive a car, they travel to other planets.

Magic can do all this, but it can do more. In the literary folktale, it often becomes a metaphor for the imagination. This is particularly true of Nesbit's stories. "The Book of Beasts," for instance, can be read as a fable about the power of imaginative art. The magic volume of its title contains colored pictures of exotic creatures, which become real when the book is left open. The little boy who finds it releases first a butterfly, then a bird of paradise, and finally a dragon that threatens to destroy the country. If any book is vivid enough, this story says, what is in it will become real to us and invade our world for good or evil.

It is imagination, disguised as magic, that gives Nesbit's characters (and by extension her readers) the power to journey through space and time: to see India or the South Seas, to visit Shakespeare's London, ancient Egypt, or a future Utopia. It will even take them to Atlantis or to a mermaid's castle under the sea. All these places, of course, are the traditional destinations of fantasy voyages, even today. But an imagination that can operate only in conventional fantasy scenery is in constant danger of becoming sentimental and escapist. At its worst, it produces the sort of mental condition that manifests itself in plastic unicorns and a Disney World version of foreign countries. True imaginative power like Nesbit's, on the other hand, is strong enough to transform the most prosaic contemporary scene, and comedy is its best ally. Nesbit's magic is as much at home in a basement in Camden Town as on a South Sea island, and it is never merely romantic. Though it grants the desires of her characters, it may also expose these desires as comically misconceived.

Five Children and It, for instance, is not only an amusing adventure story but also a tale of the vanity of human — or at least juvenile — wishes. The children first want to be "as beautiful as the day";[22] later they ask for a sand pit full of gold sovereigns, giant size and strength, and instant adulthood. Each wish leads them into an appropriate comic disaster. When they become beautiful, for instance, their baby brother does not recognize them and bursts into howls of distrust, and they begin to quarrel among themselves — a not unusual result of such transformations in real life. In every case, when the spell ends at sunset the children are greatly relieved. The reader, of course, has the pleasure of living out these granted wishes in imagination, plus the assurance that his or her unattainable desires are not so desirable after all; it is the same sort of double satisfaction that adults get from reading in *People* magazine of the discomforts of the rich and famous.

Sometimes Nesbit's magical transformations are not so much imaginative projections of what might come to pass as metaphors for the actual state of things. Often they make literal the perception that many adults have no idea of what is going on with the children who are living with them, and possibly don't even care. In *The Enchanted Castle,* for instance, Mabel finds a ring that makes her invisible; but it is clear that she was already more or less invisible to the aunt with whom she lives. Mabel's aunt feels not the slightest anxiety about her disappearance and readily swallows a made-up story about her having been adopted by a lady in a motorcar. The other children are shocked by this insouciance, but Mabel explains that her aunt's mind is clogged with sentimental fantasy: "She's not mad, only she's always reading novelettes."[23] (We would call them popular romances.)

The same kind of thing occurs in *Five Children and It*. When, as the result of an impetuous wish, the children's home is attacked by Red Indians, the cook and parlormaid remain quite unaware of what is happening. They continue to go about their domestic business with self-absorbed complacency, just as many adults do in the presence of children haunted by imagined terrors that are nevertheless real and threatening to them.

For Nesbit, comedy is the frequent ally of this sort of metaphoric magic. In "The Cockatoucan" the laughter of a magical bird transforms everything and everyone, in the process revealing their true nature. The unpleasant nursemaid Pridmore, for instance, becomes an "Automatic Nagging Machine" like the candy dispensers in London railway stations, "greedy, grasping things which take your pennies and give you next to nothing in chocolate and change."[24] (What comes out of Pridmore is little rolls of paper with remarks on them like "Don't be tiresome.") As the Cockatoucan continues to laugh, the king of the country is exposed as a vulgar, undersized fraud: "His crown grew large and brassy, and was set with cheap glass in the worst possible taste; . . . his sceptre grew twenty feet long and extremely awkward to carry."[25]

In the most striking episode of *The Enchanted Castle*, Nesbit's Fabian convictions, her comic sense, and her use of magic as a metaphor work together. Mabel and the other children decide to put on a play, and because there are only three grown-ups available to watch it, they construct the members of an audience out of old clothes, pillows, umbrellas, brooms, and hockey sticks, with painted paper faces. A magic ring brings these ungainly creatures to life, and they are transformed into awful caricatures of different types of contemporary adults. Eventually, most of the "Ugly-Wuglies" (as Gerald calls them) are disenchanted and become piles of old clothes again, but one remains alive. He is the sort of elderly gentleman "who travels first class and smokes expensive cigars,"[26] and Jimmy, the most materialistic of the children, is rather impressed by him: " 'He's got a motor-car,' Jimmy went on, . . . 'and a garden with a tennis court and a lake and a carriage and pair. . . . He's frightfully rich, . . . He's simply rolling in money. I wish I was rich.' "[27] And, since he has the magic ring, his wish is instantly granted:

> By quick but perfectly plain-to-be-seen degrees Jimmy became rich. . . . The whole thing was over in a few seconds. Yet in those few seconds they saw him grow to a youth, a young man, a middle-aged man; and then, with a sort of shivering shock, unspeakably horrible and definite, he seemed to settle down into an elderly gentleman, handsomely but rather dowdily dressed, who was looking down at them through spectacles and asking them the nearest way to the railway station. . . .
> "Oh, Jimmy, don't!" cried Mabel desperately.
> Gerald said: "This is perfectly beastly," and Kathleen broke into wild weeping.[28]

In his new persona Jimmy no longer knows the other children and is very unpleasant to them. But he turns out to be well acquainted with the elderly Ugly-Wugly, and they travel up to London together, followed by Jimmy's desperate brother Gerald. There it appears that both Jimmy and the Ugly-Wugly have offices in the City complete with "a tangle of clerks and mahogany desks."[29] An office boy tells Gerald

that in spite of their apparent friendship, the two stockbrokers
"is all for cutting each other's throats — oh, only in the way
of business — been at it for years."[30]

The whole episode plunges Gerald into a kind of exis-
tential crisis:

> [He] wildly wondered what magic and how much had
> been needed to give history and a past to these two
> things of yesterday, the rich Jimmy and the Ugly-Wugly.
> If he could get them away would all memory of them
> fade — in this boy's mind, for instance, in the minds of
> all the people who did business with them in the City?
> Would the mahogany-and-clerk-furnished offices fade
> away? Were the clerks real? Was the mahogany? Was
> he himself real?[31]

Since Gerald is a character in a book, the answer to
this last question is no. He is literally no realer than the elderly
Ugly-Wugly — he too is a creature composed playfully out
of odds and ends and imagined into life. But however unreal
Gerald may be, Nesbit is clearly suggesting, there is something even more unreal about the successful City man. Essentially, in spite of the pomps and circumstances of his
exterior life, he is, as Gerald puts it, "only just old clothes
and nothing inside."[32] He is an empty assemblage of expensive tailoring — and/or a greedy little boy who has grown up
too fast.

It is also possible to see the magic in Nesbit's tales as
a metaphor for her own art. In many of her fantasies the
children begin by using supernatural power in a casual, materialistic way: to get money and to play tricks on people.
Gradually they find better uses for magic: in *The Story of the
Amulet,* to unite the souls of an ancient and a modern scholar,
and at the end of *The Enchanted Castle,* to reveal the unity
of all created things. Nesbit, similarly, first used her talents

to produce hackwork and pay the bills; only much later did she come to respect her gift and write the books for which she is still remembered.

Nesbit's magic can also be read as a metaphor for imaginative literature in general. Those who possess supernatural abilities or literary gifts, like the Psammead of *Five Children and It*, are not necessarily attractive or good-tempered; they may be ugly, cross, or ridiculous. We do not know who will be moved by even the greatest works of art, nor how long their power will last; and the duration and effect of magic in Nesbit's stories are unpredictable in the same way. Certain sorts of people remain untouched by it, and it is often suspected of being a dream, a delusion, or a lie. The episode of the Ugly-Wuglies also suggests that things carelessly given life by the imagination may become frightening and dangerous; the writer may be destroyed by his or her second-rate creations — by the inferior work that survives to debase reputation, or by some casual production that catches the popular imagination and types its creator forever.

Also, though they were written eighty years ago, Nesbit's books express a common anxiety of writers today: that the contemporary world, with its speed of travel and new methods of communication, will soon have no use for literature. As practical Jimmy puts it in *The Enchanted Castle:* "I think magic went out when people began to have steam engines, . . . and newspapers, and telephones and wireless telegraphing."[33]

NEW AS Nesbit's stories are in comparison with most children's books of her period, in some ways they also look back to the oldest sort of juvenile literature, the traditional folktale. They recall the simplicity and directness of diction, and the physical humor, of the folktale rather than the poetic language, intellectual wit, and didactic intention of the typical Victorian fairy tale.

Socially, too, Nesbit's stories have affinities with folklore. Her adventurous little girls and athletic princesses recall the many traditional tales in which the heroines have wit, courage, and strength. And there is also a parallel with her political stance. The classic folktales first recorded by scholars in the nineteenth century tend to view the world from a working-class perspective — not unnaturally, since most of them were collected from uneducated farmers, servants, and artisans. The heroes and heroines of these tales are usually the children of poor people. When they go out into the world to seek their fortunes they confront supernatural representatives of the upper classes: rich, ugly giants and magicians and ogres. Many of these tales also, like Nesbit's, make fun of establishment figures.

There is no way of knowing whether E. Nesbit went back to these traditional models consciously, or whether it was her own attitude toward the world that made her break so conclusively with the past. Whatever the explanation, she managed not only to create some of the best children's books ever written, but to quietly popularize ideas about society and about childhood that were, in her time, extremely subversive. Today, when the works of writers like Mrs. Ewing and Mrs. Molesworth and Mrs. Craik are gathering dust on the shelves of secondhand bookshops, her stories are still read and loved by children, and imitated by adults.

10

The Boy Who Couldn't Grow Up

JAMES BARRIE

In every society, every century, some time of life seems to embody current cultural ideals and have superior prestige. In ancient China, we are told, the greatest honor was given to old age; America in the 1960s admired teenagers, attributing to them boundless energy, political altruism, and a polymorphously joyous sensuality.

The Victorians, on the other hand, preferred children who had not yet reached puberty. The natural innocents of Blake and Wordsworth reappeared in middlebrow versions in hundreds of nineteenth-century stories and poems, always uncannily good and sensitive, with an angelic beauty and charm that often move the angels to carry them off. But the early death of these children was not felt as wholly tragic, for if they never became adults they would escape worldly sin and suffering; they would remain forever pure and happy. It seems quite appropriate that a man walking in London's Kensington Gardens near the Albert Memorial, in the final years of Victoria's reign, should have imagined the last and most famous of these unaging innocents: Peter Pan, the Boy Who Wouldn't Grow Up.

The current view of *Peter Pan* as a shallow, cloyingly

cute fantasy is probably based on memories of the Disney film, or some similarly oversimplified and oversugared version of the story on the stage or in print. The original play is far more interesting and complicated, just as its author, James Barrie, was a more original and complex man than he is now generally reputed to be.

Current opinion is not absolutely wrong: Barrie was a whimsical romantic with an emotional, occasionally a maudlin, devotion to mothers and children. But he was also a shrewd, cynical, and highly successful journalist and dramatist who had made his way from a weaver's cottage in a remote Scottish village to a town house in South Kensington. As the seventh of eight surviving children, and the adopted uncle of five more, he knew very well that juvenile charm and innocence are often accompanied by profound egotism and an unconscious capacity for cruelty. Moreover, Barrie knew, for the most bitter and private reasons, what a boy who didn't grow up would really be like. He was that boy. His strange story echoes through nearly all his writing, but it can be heard most clearly in his memoir of his mother, *Margaret Ogilvy* (1896), and his two remarkable and now almost unknown autobiographical novels, *Sentimental Tommy* (1896) and *Tommy and Grizel* (1900).

For the first six years of his life, Jamie Barrie seems to have been an ordinary little boy, not unusually good or unusually clever; an unimportant member of his large, impoverished family. The center of attention was James's brilliant older brother David. David was unmistakably his parents' favorite and the focus of his mother's ambition; she was determined that he would win a scholarship to Edinburgh University and become a famous minister — "the highest reward on earth any mother could hope for."[1]

But on the day before his fourteenth birthday David was

killed in a skating accident. The entire family was demoralized, and upon hearing the news his mother took to her bed with grief. She stayed there for more than a year, refusing at first to eat or speak. Jamie's oldest sister, upon whom all the work of the household had devolved, found him sitting crying on the stairs one day and told him to go in to his mother "and say to her that she still had another boy."

> The room was dark, and when I heard the door shut and no sound come from the bed I was afraid, and I stood still. . . . after a time I heard a listless voice . . . say, "Is that you?" . . . I thought it was the dead boy she was speaking to, and I said in a little lonely voice, "No, it's no' him, it's just me."[2]

During the months that followed, Jamie spent most of his waking hours in his mother's room, sitting on her bed and trying to comfort and cheer her. He conceived "an intense desire" to take the place of his dead brother, "to become so like him that even my mother should not see the difference."[3] He promised her that he too would be a famous man, and make her as proud as David would have done.

In *Margaret Ogilvy*, written just after his mother's death, Barrie relates the story in full but without any apparent recognition that it is a very odd one, or that readers might question statements such as "Nothing that happens after we are twelve matters very much."[4] His mother appears as an unusually original, imaginative, and charming woman; he seems unaware that he is also describing someone of terrifying ambition and a pathologically jealous possessiveness.

Barrie got his wish and kept his vow to his mother — but with a curious fairy tale twist. He became a famous man, and, in a peculiar, awful way, he became David: David exactly as he had been on the day he died. Though he grew older, James Barrie never quite grew up. He remained for the rest of his long life a brilliant boy just short of puberty whose greatest pleasure was in children's stories and games and whose deepest attachment was to his mother.

The resemblance was more than psychological. Barrie was also a boy in appearance: barely over five feet tall, extremely slight and youthful, with a thin, small voice. In photographs taken during his twenties and early thirties he looks like a thirteen-year-old wearing a false mustache. And though given to romantic crushes on pretty women, he was apparently incapable of physical love. His marriage at thirty-four, to a young actress in his first hit play, was probably never consummated.

It is possible that Barrie's inability to mature was physical rather than — or as well as — psychological. Dr. James Purdom-Martin, a London physician who has made a lifelong study of such cases, believes that Barrie may have suffered from delayed or incomplete puberty, perhaps related to a glandular deficiency.[5] Milder forms of this condition, according to Dr. Purdom-Martin, are fairly common; today they are often corrected by hormone shots. In extreme instances, the voice does not deepen, facial and body hair do not develop, and the sexual parts fail to mature; the adult man remains physiologically a boy of twelve or thirteen. The causes are not fully understood, but it is conceivable, such is the complex interconnection of mind and body, that some people may be able to choose not to grow up, like Peter Pan, though perhaps not so consciously.

Intellectually, however, the young James Barrie was anyone's equal. He graduated from Edinburgh University in 1883 and rapidly became a successful journalist and essayist. In his midtwenties he moved to London and began to publish semifictional stories and novels about village life in Scotland, which combined a delicate sense of comedy with a deep love of the scenes and characters of his youth.

Tommy Sandys, the hero of Barrie's unexpectedly serious and psychologically subtle autobiographical novels, *Sentimental Tommy* and *Tommy and Grizel,* is also a boy who cannot grow up. As a child he is gifted, inventive, and affectionate; he brings happiness and interest into everyone's life. As a man he lies to his friends and drives the woman who loves him temporarily insane, though in the end (unlike Barrie's wife, who finally left him for a young lawyer) she forgives and accepts him: "He did not love her. 'Not as I love him,' she said to herself. 'Not as married people ought to love, but in the other way he loves me dearly.' . . . He was a boy who could not grow up."[6]

Tommy, who was "so fond of boyhood that he could not with years become a man,"[7] is not only like Barrie in being a perpetual boy; he is also a Scotsman and a successful writer. The books in which he appears give a devastating portrait of the artist as unconscious phony. The narrative tone throughout has nothing of the soapy whimsy associated with Barrie's name — it is that of his other self, the coolly ironic London journalist.

From an early age Tommy has the writer's trick of turning the people and events around him into material for his fantasies. That Barrie was well aware of this habit in himself a passage from his notebook shows: "Scene: Husband taking notes of wife's quaintness, &c., for novel. Her indignation — a quarrel — till he promises never to do it again. (Then he takes a note of this!)"[8]

Tommy is also an inspired liar and fantast for whom the world of his imagination is realer than the drab, untidy one he lives in. He romanticizes everyone, including himself, and every situation; before he is ten he talks his way into a charity banquet by pretending to be a reformed juvenile delinquent and even convinces himself: "When he described the eerie darkness of the butler's pantry, he shivered involuntarily, and he shut his eyes once — ugh! — that was because he saw the blood spouting out of the butler."[9]

As an adult Tommy is unchanged. Out on a walk one day, he begins to limp painfully when he thinks of a story about a man with a wooden leg. His friends notice and ask solicitously if he is hurt. Tommy is so taken by their sympathy and the possibilities of the part of stoical wounded hero that he ends up with a real sprained ankle.

More seriously, when he sees that Grizel is in love with him, Tommy at once begins to imagine and then to play out a series of heavy romantic scenes with her. "For instance, if she would only let him love her hopelessly. . . . how finely he would behave. It would bring out all that was best in him. 'Is there no hope for me?' He heard himself begging for hope, and he heard also her firm answer, 'None.' . . . (How charmingly it was all working out.)"[10] Unfortunately Grizel is happy to give Tommy hope, and he plays along, gradually getting carried away by his own rhetoric: "He so loved the thing he had created that in his exaltation he mistook it for her. He believed all he was saying. He looked at her long and adoringly, not, as he thought, because he adored her, but because it was thus that look should answer look; . . . he was the artist trying in a mad moment to be as well as to do."[11]

Presently Tommy comes to his senses, realizes he has talked himself into an engagement he cannot fulfill, and rejects Grizel cruelly. He then runs away to London, where he writes a very sentimental — and very successful — book about unrequited love.

Tommy's self-dramatization is interesting partly because it is an exaggerated version of something most people have done at one time or another. Not many of us get into such serious trouble; but who reading this essay can swear they never improved an anecdote, or spoke a line because it went well with the scenery?

Four years later Barrie told his story again, but this time, like Tommy Sandys, he turned it inside out. The boy who could not with years become a man was transformed into the boy who refuses to become a man — Peter Pan. The emphasis was no longer on loss and pain and deception, but on pleasure and discovery.

This new perspective was the result of a profound change in Barrie's life. *Sentimental Tommy* was written from within a failed and unreal marriage, *Peter Pan* out of the longest and most intense relationship of Barrie's adulthood. It began one day in 1897, when he was walking his Saint Bernard, Porthos, in Kensington Gardens. The tiny man and the huge dog made friends with two little boys, George and Jack Davies, then aged five and four, who were playing in the park, accompanied by their nurse and baby brother. Soon they were meeting almost every day. Barrie, who loved children, was a delightful companion; he played exciting games with the boys and told them wonderful stories. Many of his tales were about what happened in Kensington Gardens after they closed for the night, and one of the characters in them was Peter Pan. He was a boy who had flown away from his nursery because he didn't want to grow up. He lived on an island in the Serpentine, where he slept in a nest made out of a five-pound note lost by the poet Shelley, and was friends with birds and fairies.[12] He was thus imaginatively connected with poetic creation as well as with the romantic imagination. (It is perhaps worth recalling that Percy Shelley, like James Barrie, was an extremely small, boyish-looking man.)

At a London dinner party later that year, Barrie was introduced to the boys' parents, Arthur and Sylvia Davies. Gradually he became a regular guest at their house and a kind of adopted uncle to the Davies children. When they met, the Davies already had three young sons, and Sylvia later gave birth to two more. As the younger boys grew up, they too became friends and playmates of Barrie's.[13]

From the start the reactions of the family to Barrie varied. The boys were enchanted by him, and their mother, Sylvia, was tolerant, though she regarded Barrie's growing romantic crush on her with amused indifference. But Arthur Davies, a hardworking young barrister, did not care for the odd little man with the plebeian Scots accent who seemed to be spending most of his waking hours in Arthur's house, paying extravagant compliments to Arthur's wife and playing with Arthur's children.

But apparently he couldn't do much about it. The constant visits and stories and games and presents continued, breaking off only in the summers; and in 1901 the Davieses rented a country cottage on Black Lake in Surrey for the holidays almost next door to the Barries' cottage. For six weeks they saw each other almost every day. Barrie was forty-one that summer, but he still looked more like an adolescent boy than a grown man; and he was apparently accepted as such by the Davies boys (there were four now, one still a baby). To them he seemed like a wonderfully clever older brother, the inventor and leader of exciting games in the woods and on the shores of the lake — games involving pirates, Indians, shipwrecks, and desert islands.

Barrie recorded these adventures with a camera, and after the holidays were over he made his photographs into an album titled *The Boy Castaways of Black Lake Island*. The book had imaginary chapter headings and seriocomic captions ("We prepared for the pirates by making spears and other trusty weapons"). There were two copies, but only one survives; Arthur Davies, the boys' father, almost immediately left the other one in a train.

By this time Barrie had already begun a third career,

as a dramatist. His plays were even more successful than his fiction; some of them, like *The Admirable Crichton* (1902) and *What Every Woman Knows* (1908), are still occasionally performed today. *Peter Pan*, begun in 1903, is on its simplest level a combination of the stories he told the Davies children in Kensington Gardens and the games he invented for them in Surrey. The Never Land (later, and with sadder finality, the Never-Never Land) is the place where all these stories and games can come true at once. But the play is much more than this. In its outward form, it is a classic English Christmas pantomime, which appropriately had its first performance in London on December 27, 1904.

A pantomime in British theatrical tradition is not a silent, mimed play, but a kind of musical comedy for children. In the early years of this century such shows were widely performed at the Christmas holidays, as they still are today. They were usually based on well-known folktales or children's classics: *Robinson Crusoe,* "Jack and the Beanstalk," "Ali Baba and the Forty Thieves," "Puss in Boots," *Mother Goose,* and so on. A pantomime had several stock characters: a young hero and heroine, the Principal Boy and Principal Girl, both always played by young actresses; the Good Fairy (and sometimes a Bad Fairy as well); the principal villain, or Demon King; and the Dame, an old woman portrayed by a male comic in drag.

Another important feature of the classic pantomime was the so-called transformation scene in which through stage magic the everyday world of the first act was changed into a kind of fairyland. There were songs and dances, fights and flights — the last being managed by suspending the actors and actresses from invisible wires.

Like *Mother Goose, Dick Whittington,* or *Aladdin, Peter Pan* presents a medley of incongruous fantasy settings — the mermaids' lagoon, the forest full of wolves and Indians, the pirate ship. There are music, songs, dancing, and a trans-formation scene; a chorus of children (the Lost Boys) appears. The original production of *Peter Pan* even ended with the then-traditional harlequinade.

The conventional pantomime characters are all in-cluded. Peter Pan (always played by a young woman in tights, according to tradition) is the Principal Boy — youthful, imag-inative, courageous, somewhat boastful. Wendy is the Prin-cipal Girl, full of gentle, innocent feminine charm. Captain Hook is the Demon King, and Nana, the dog-nurse (usually played by a man), is the Dame. Peter fights the traditional third-act duel, with Captain Hook, and the standard trans-formation scene occurs in the flight to Never-Never Land, when the walls of the nursery set melt away into the wings, revealing the London skyline and a sky full of stars. *Peter Pan* even observes the pantomime tradition, inherited from the old mystery and morality plays, that the villains enter from stage left and the good characters from stage right.

Among Barrie's innovations was the fairy Tinker Bell, who appears only as a moving light and a silvery ringing. She is both the Good Fairy and the Bad Fairy: loving and pro-tective toward Peter, murderously jealous of Wendy. Anyone who has seen the play will remember the famous moment in which Tinker Bell is dying and Peter calls on everyone in the theater who believes in fairies to save her by clapping their hands. This scene was originally a great source of anxiety to Barrie: on opening night (and on many later occasions) he walked about nervously at the back of the auditorium, waiting to see if the audience would answer Peter's appeal.* After what always seemed to him a long pause, they responded overwhelmingly, and have done so ever since. The idea was

---

*On the first night the producer, equally worried, placed a claque in the theater in case no one should applaud.

not only wonderfully original and effective, it was a brilliant dramatic metaphor; for of course ultimately all characters in literature are kept alive by the belief of readers and playgoers.

But *Peter Pan* is much more than a conventional pantomime. Its Never-Never Land is the world of childhood imagination; it is also a refuge from the adult universe of rules and duties. It is peopled with a jumble of characters from the games Barrie played with the Davies boys: a pirate ship and crew, a band of Red Indians, wild animals, fairies, mermaids. It features two classic locales of romance — a desert island and an underground hideout. Peter Pan, the boy who has refused to grow up, is among other things an incarnation of the Greek god Pan, who figures so often in late Victorian and Edwardian literature.[14] There, as in classical tradition, he was a spirit of the woods who embodied natural energy and sexual passion, and was represented as a man with goat's legs and pointed ears, playing on a reed pipe. Barrie's Pan, however, is a child who plays pipes and rides a goat.

Beyond all this, *Peter Pan* is an allegory of Barrie's relations with the Davies family. All the names of the male Davieses are in the play, and the name Wendy, never known until then, was taken from the mispronunciation of another young friend of Barrie's, Margaret Henley, who had died at the age of six; she had called herself Barrie's "friendy" but had trouble with her consonants. Mrs. Darling, whose given name in the play is Mary, is partly Sylvia Davies, whom Barrie loved and admired as the perfect mother. But in another, sadder way she is Barrie's wife, Mary, to whom he now in imagination gives the children she had longed to have.

Mrs. Darling is "the loveliest lady in Bloomsbury."[15] Mr. Darling, on the other hand, is a coward and a bully and a hypocrite. (It is worth noting that in production the same actor customarily doubles as Mr. Darling and Captain Hook.) He cons his son Michael into taking nasty medicine by pretending to take some even nastier medicine of his own, and then instead pours it into Nana's bowl. When his family does not appreciate this, Mr. Darling rapidly becomes hysterical:

> MR. DARLING. It was only a joke. Much good my wearing myself to the bone trying to be funny in this house.
>
> WENDY (*on her knees by the kennel*). Father, Nana is crying.
>
> MR. DARLING. Coddle her; nobody coddles me. Oh dear no. I am only the bread-winner, why should I be coddled? Why, why, why?[16]

That is what you get for leaving people's precious photograph albums in trains.

Wendy, the "little mother," may also be an idealized version of Sylvia Davies. But the child-mother character goes back much further, to Barrie's own mother's childhood as he described it in *Margaret Ogilvy:* "She was eight when her mother's death made her mistress of the house and mother to her little brother, and from that time she scrubbed and mended and baked and sewed."[17] (Grizel in *Sentimental Tommy* is also a little mother, who keeps house for orphaned Tommy and his sister.) When Wendy reattaches Peter's shadow, what is symbolized, according to Harry M. Geduld, is the wish for Margaret Ogilvy to fuse her dead and her living son.*

As for Peter Pan himself, many writers have seen him as a supernatural incarnation of Barrie himself; eternally young in spirit, the ideal companion and daring leader in child-

---

*Geduld's critical study of Barrie's work (1971) contains many such interesting if not invariably convincing insights. It is somewhat handicapped by adherence to a rigidly psychoanalytic system of interpretation, and more seriously by Geduld's not having been able for some reason to consult Janet Dunbar's excellent and definitive biography, *J. M. Barrie: The Man Behind the Image* (1970).

hood games. But he is also, as Barrie could not be, a real child. Others have identified Peter with Barrie's brother David, who can never grow older and lives underground with the Lost Boys in what may be a land of the dead.*

Though Peter is less powerful than the Greek god Pan, he is not without his dark side. Barrie remarks in the fictionalized version of his play, *Peter and Wendy,* that children are "gay and innocent and heartless,"[18] and Peter is all of these. He is forgetful, naively self-centered, and inconstant — most strikingly in the epilogue Barrie added to *Peter and Wendy.* Here Peter comes back to the nursery twenty years later, rejects the weeping, grown-up Wendy, and flies off to Never-Never Land with her daughter Jane.

An even darker side of Barrie's vision appears in the character of Captain Hook, who significantly also turns out to be named James and shares his inventor's fondness for cigars. The crocodile that follows Captain Hook, relentlessly ticking (it has swallowed a clock as well as Hook's right hand), is one of the wittiest and most sinister symbols ever created of the way all of us except Peter Pan are stalked by devouring Time. It is perhaps especially terrifying to those who cling to their lost childhood and youth. The plot of acts 2 through 5 turns on the rivalry between Peter and Hook for the possession of Wendy. Not possession in the physical sense: in spite of his name, Peter Pan is completely asexual. "You mustn't touch me," he cries in the final published version of the script. "No one must ever touch me."[19] He asks Wendy to come to Never-Never Land so that she may be a mother to him and the Lost Boys. Hook, too, wants to kidnap Wendy only so that he and the other pirates may have a mother.

*The Lost Boys, according to the play, are children who fall out of their perambulators when the nurse is looking the other way; it should also be remembered that in a euphemism of the time still in use today, to say that someone had "lost" a relative meant that this person had died.

In fact, Peter Pan and Captain Hook are not so much opposites as two sides of the same coin. After Peter has defeated Hook in their final duel there is a tableau; Barrie writes in the stage directions, "The curtain rises to show Peter a very Napoleon on his ship. It must not rise again lest we see him on the poop in Hook's hat and cigars, and with a small iron claw."[20]

According to Peter Davies, whenever Barrie "was strongly attracted by people, he wanted at once to own them . . . whichever their sex."[21] Assuming that what Barrie wanted in 1904 was to own Sylvia Davies and her sons, it is possible to see Peter Pan as the innocent embodiment of this desire and Captain Hook as the guilty one.

In *Peter Pan* every wish comes true, from early fantasies of flying to the resurrection of the dead: the Lost Boys, missing, possibly dead children who live underground in a sort of cozy tomb, finally return to London, where they are adopted by the Darlings. The whole play is an elaborate dream fulfillment of intense but contradictory childhood wishes — to be grown up at once and never to be grown up; to have exciting adventures and be perfectly safe; to escape from your mother and have her always at hand. It is also, in some sense, deeply subversive, in that it demonstrates graphically that parents are timid and hypocritical and that it is far better to be young and live in Never-Never Land.

No wonder that *Peter Pan* was received with overwhelming enthusiasm and that it has become the most famous children's play ever written, as well as the greatest success in recent British stage history: it was performed more than ten thousand times in England alone between 1904 and 1954, according to Roger Lancelyn Green's entertaining record of this success, *Fifty Years of Peter Pan*. Admiration for the play has reached odd heights at times. Its first producer, the American showman Charles Frohman, who was killed in the sinking of the *Lusitania,* is reported to have cried as the ship went down, "To die will be an awfully big adventure!" — Peter's curtain line in act 3.

IN *Peter Pan* the story ends with the return of the children to their parents. But in real life the outcome was stranger. Again, just as in childhood, Barrie got his wish, and again in an awful way. In 1906 Arthur Davies was suddenly found to have cancer, and within a year he was dead. He left five sons, aged two to fourteen, and very little money. James Barrie, who was now a rich man, stepped into the breach. He became the main — and very generous — support of the family and their constant companion.

A happy ending, for him at least? Briefly, perhaps. But the crocodile was still there offstage, slowly but fatally moving closer. The Davies boys were effectively Barrie's now; but they would not remain boys. One by one, as they grew older, they began to find his games and jokes embarrassing and to resent his presence in the household — an embarrassment and resentment complicated by the knowledge that this strange little man who looked like an aged child was paying the tradesmen's bills and their fees at Eton and Oxford.

Barrie was well aware of these feelings. He wrote during a later holiday with some of the boys and their school friends: "We are a very Etonian household and there is endless shop talked, during which I am expected to be merely a ladler out of food. If I speak to one he shudders politely then edges away."[22]

Worse still was to come. In 1910 Sylvia Davies herself died, and the grief-stricken Barrie found himself responsible for five lost boys, three of whom were now definitely too old to play pirates. A few years later George, the eldest Davies boy, was killed in World War I in France, and Peter invalided home with severe shell shock. The perfect family of which Barrie had been an adopted member was scattered.

By the time the war ended even the youngest of the remaining Davies boys was too old to play with Barrie. He was still a famous man, but he had written nothing much for several years and was beginning to fear that he would never do any serious work again. He had an idea for a new play; when he began to make notes for it, however, he developed a severe writer's cramp and pain in his right hand and arm, in a late and uncanny imitation of Captain Hook. Since he found it nearly impossible to dictate, it seemed likely that this was the end of his career.

But lonely and distressed as he was, Barrie still had remarkable strength of will. With some difficulty, he trained himself to write with his left hand and went on with the new play, *Mary Rose*. His affliction, he remarked, had made him into two authors; the new work, done with the left hand, "was more sinister."[23]

And in spite of some passages of sentimentality, *Mary Rose* is in many ways a sinister play, a final and darker version of *Peter Pan*. There is an enchanted island, a lost boy, temporarily bereaved parents, and children who never grow up; but the mood of the play is not joyous; it is melancholy and weird, even frightening. It was based on old Scottish legends Barrie heard as a child, in which mortals are stolen away to fairyland and return days or years later with no memory of where they have been.

Mary Rose is the only child of a nice but rather timid and silly English couple who love her so much they can't bear for her to grow up. In a way they have already gotten their wish when the play opens. Years earlier, when Mary Rose was eleven, she vanished on an island in the Hebrides during a vacation trip. Her parents believed her drowned, but instead she reappeared twenty days later in the same spot, unaware that any time had passed. At eighteen she is remarkably immature for her age, and childishly dependent both on her parents and on the young man to whom she has become engaged.

Act 2 takes place four or five years later on the island. Mary Rose is now married and the mother of a son but still very immature emotionally — the last and saddest of Barrie's little-girl mothers. Though she is perfectly happy, she hates the idea that her baby will grow up or that she and her husband will grow old. Again, the island grants the wish. Mary Rose disappears while her husband's back is turned, only this time she is gone for twenty-five years. When she finally reappears, looking not a day older, without any memory of the intervening years and eager to see her baby son again, she is a source of great distress and embarrassment to her middle-aged husband and elderly parents.

In the last act of the play Mary Rose, now dead, appears as a ghost haunting her deserted house. She is pathetically childish, doubly bereaved because she has not only lost her parents and her little boy but is losing her memories of them and even her own identity. When her son, now a young man, appears, she does not know him and even wants to kill him:

> HARRY.   Where is my knife? Were you standing look-
>   ing at me with my knife in your hand? *(She is sullenly
>   silent.)* Give me my knife. *(She gives it to him.)* What
>   made you take it?
> MARY ROSE.   I thought perhaps you were the one.
> HARRY.   The one?
> MARY ROSE.   The one who stole him from me.[24]

Mary Rose is all the women Barrie has loved and lost: his childless wife, Mary; Sylvia Davies, now dead; and his own mother, who could never forget her son David and became similarly childish before her death. And Mary Rose is also Barrie himself, ghostlike and ageless in a changed world — a world in which his parents are dead and the little boys he loved have turned into strange and hateful young men.

To quote Mr. Geduld, who says some of these things and many more, "the 'message' in *Mary Rose* can be expressed . . . as the conviction that to attempt to hold back the clock, to deny the future for the sake of the past, is the pursuit of a fantasy that ultimately destroys the pursuer."[25]

Though *Mary Rose* was a stage success in 1920, it puzzled audiences and critics and is now practically unknown. Which is too bad, for it has particular application today. It is no longer so popular in America to be adolescent: the fashionable age now seems to be about thirty. Because of the postwar baby boom, America is now full of people this age — and of somewhat older people pretending to be about the same age.

When youth is so favored, it is natural to want to be young; but the effort to seem so, if too long continued, is exhausting and demoralizing. And when the refusal to grow up, or to grow old, becomes absolute, the effects are terrifying. In extreme cases of Peter Pan syndrome your closest friends and relatives are forgotten, just as Peter forgot Wendy; memory and even identity lapse. What finally remains is one of those attractive, energetic, ageless, youngish people we all know, with the same dazed and accusing look in their eyes you can see in some of the late photographs of Barrie, the look he saw at the end in the eyes of Mary Rose.

11

Happy Endings

FRANCES HODGSON BURNETT

A few writers produce what economists call consumer durables. Their works, like a house or a silver teapot or a Grecian urn, will last a lifetime and often longer. Other authors, the great majority, manufacture "soft goods" — sometimes highly profitable but hastily and flimsily made, intended to be used and thrown out. They may be courted by publishers and booksellers and receive a lot of fan mail, but after their death, or even sooner, they are forgotten. They are not mentioned in biographical dictionaries, and their books molder unread in the spare bedrooms of country cottages.

For most of her lifetime Frances Hodgson Burnett was this second sort of writer. Her sentimental magazine stories and romantic novels were the Victorian equivalent of acrylic sweaters and paper plates. She is remembered now, when authors like Elizabeth Ward and Mrs. E.D.E.N. Southworth are forgotten, because at least twice in more than half a century of constant and often exhausting commercial productivity (fifty-four published books and thirteen stage plays) she happened to tell one of those stories that express concealed fantasies and longings; stories that are the externalized dreams of a whole society and pass beyond ordinary commercial success to become part of popular culture.

Mrs. Burnett's first dream, *Little Lord Fauntleroy* (1886), was a book-length version of the almost universal childhood fantasy that one doesn't really belong in this dreary little house or flat with these boring, ordinary people — that one's real parents are important and exciting and live in a great mansion, if not a castle. Marghanita Laski has remarked that the standard Frances Hodgson Burnett plot is one in which a disadvantaged person, often a child, is restored to the wealth and position which are his natural birthrights. Sara Crewe is rescued from her garret; Emily Fox-Seton, in *The Making of a Marchioness,* marries a peer who has recognized the true lady behind the paid companion; little Cedric, living in reduced circumstances with his widowed mother in New York, is discovered to be Lord Fauntleroy, the heir of the earl of Dorincourt.

It was of course a common theme in Victorian romantic fiction, and a very natural one for Mrs. Burnett, whose own life had a riches-to-rags-to-riches outline. She was born in Manchester in 1840, one of five children of a prosperous tradesman. When she was three years old her father died, plunging the family into shabby-genteel poverty, first in England and then in rural Tennessee, to which they emigrated in 1865, when Frances was fifteen. She was a clever, independent, bossy, and rather plain young girl, small, pudgy, and red-haired, with a gift for storytelling.*

---

*Until recently Frances Hodgson Burnett has had bad luck with biographers. Her son's *The Romantick Lady,* like most sentimental hagiographies, positively invites irritated skepticism. It seems to have had that effect on Marghanita Laski, who in *Mrs. Ewing, Mrs. Molesworth, and Mrs. Hodgson Burnett* describes her third subject as "aggressively domineering, offensively whimsical, and abominably self-centered and conceited. She had a kind of tough vulgarity which led her to see herself continually as a heroine." Luckily, Ann Thwaite found this unflattering portrait of one of her favorite childhood authors hard to believe, and she set out deliberately to discover more. The Frances Hodgson Burnett who emerges from her biography is an interesting and largely sympathetic character.

The account of her American girlhood in Ann Thwaite's excellent biography reads like a chapter from *Little Women:* family picnics and parties, made-over frocks and constant, usually unsuccessful attempts to earn money in small ways:

> They tried everything in those early days. Embroidery — and people didn't want it. Music lessons — and people thought them too young. Chickens — and they wouldn't hatch, and when they did they died of the gapes. There was the awful problem, too, of having to sit on the hen to make her sit on the nest. They tried setting goose eggs and only one hatched and that wasn't a goose. It was a gander, and a plank fell on it and killed it.[1]

Frances Hodgson, like Louisa May Alcott, wrote her way out of this predicament, at first without any serious literary ambitions. "My object is remuneration," she wrote in the letter she sent to a second-rate women's magazine when she was seventeen, along with her first story.[2] ("It would have seemed to me a kind of presumption to aspire to entering the world of actual literature," she remarked much later.[3])

Frances Hodgson's story was published, and the next, and the next. Gradually she became more successful and more confident. By the time she was twenty-two, in 1872, she had earned enough by writing "five or six little ten or twelve dollar stories a month"[4] to return to England as a tourist — the first of many visits. By 1881 she was a well-known popular novelist living in considerable luxury with her husband and children in Washington, D.C., almost next door to their friend President James Garfield.

It was quite natural that she should turn to writing juveniles. She liked children and always got on well with them; she loved playing games and had a lifelong fascination with

dollhouses. Even in her adult fiction, favorite characters of
every age are described as "child-like"; and as Ann Thwaite
points out, "many of the most strongly loving relationships
are between mother and son, father and daughter, between
sisters, between friends."[5] She was less interested in love
between men and women — and less successful at it in real
life. Both her marriages ended in separation and mutual bitterness.

Mrs. Burnett was also an enthusiastic and devoted
mother who greatly admired both her sons. The character of
Cedric, Lord Fauntleroy, was consciously based on her
younger son, Vivian — who in spite of his name and the bad
press his double has received seems to have been a perfectly
normal little boy, quite reasonably noisy, grubby, and active.
Even Cedric himself is by no means the prig and sissy he is
assumed to be by people who haven't read the book. Part of
the prejudice against him is probably due to the Little Lord
Fauntleroy costume, which so many unhappy English and
American boys were forced into at the end of the last century,
although Vivian and Lionel Burnett wore such clothes only
for parties and at the photographer's.

Mrs. Burnett's stroke of genius in *Little Lord Fauntleroy*
was to combine the story of a long-lost heir with two other
equally popular contemporary subjects. One is the relation
between England and America; between an old, complex,
possibly corrupt nation and its younger, simpler, cruder, but
presumably more innocent former colony. In the years after
the Civil War, when America was finally coming of age and
(like other adolescents) beginning to forgive and feel curious
about its progenitors, American writers, and their characters,
traveled to Europe in great numbers — not only to see the
sights, but to meet Europeans, particularly Englishmen.
Sometimes, as in Mark Twain's *Innocents Abroad* (1869),
they clashed head-on. Other authors, like Henry James, ap-

proached England and the English with an infinitely anxious sidelong fascination. Mrs. Burnett, perhaps because of her childhood memories, or perhaps just through natural optimism, embraced them with romantic eagerness.

The other popular theme in *Little Lord Fauntleroy* is that of the regeneration of an older person through the influence of an affectionate and attractive child, a Wordsworthian natural innocent; the best-known British example of this genre, of course, is *Silas Marner*. England, the past, age, rank, and selfish pride are all represented, with thematic economy, by Cedric's grandfather, the fabulously rich earl of Dorincourt.

The plot of *Little Lord Fauntleroy* recalls not only George Eliot but James's *The Portrait of a Lady*, published five years earlier, in 1881, which also features the confrontation between a charming, eager, natural young American and representatives of an older and more devious civilization. In fact, the earl is in more ways than one a sort of Gilbert Osmond grown old — "In all his long life he had never really loved anyone but himself; he had been selfish and self-indulgent and arrogant and passionate."[6] But in Mrs. Burnett's story the warmhearted young hero converts the cold English aristocrat.

Frances Hodgson Burnett preferred happy endings, in life as well as in art. "There ought to be a tremendous lot of natural splendid happiness in the life of every human being,"[7] she once wrote, and she worked generously to bring this about. With the profits from her books she bought a house in Manchester, England, for distant cousins, and another in London for the impoverished spinster ladies whose school she had gone to as a child. She rented a grand country place in Kent with seven reception rooms and eighteen bedrooms, filled it with guests, and played the part of a local lady of the manor, visiting cottages and giving treats to the village children, with great success.

Mrs. Burnett's attempts to spread joy went far beyond this. Stephen Townesend, the doctor who later became her second husband, had always said he wanted to be a professional actor, so she wrote and produced a play for him to star in. Surprised and hurt by his lack of enthusiasm and gratitude, she was still determined that he should succeed.

Even in the most tragic circumstances Mrs. Burnett strove to create happiness. When her elder son became fatally ill with tuberculosis she brought him expensive toys from London shops. She sat by his bedside day and night, always calm and cheerful, strenuously and passionately determined that Lionel should not learn that there was anything serious the matter with him.

The conviction that every life should be full of "natural splendid happiness" is one of the driving forces behind Mrs. Burnett's other famous dream, *The Secret Garden* (1911). Like *Little Lord Fauntleroy*, it is about a psychological miracle: the complete regeneration of two thoroughly unpleasant and self-centered children. At the beginning of the book Mary, who lives with her parents in India, is described thus: "Everybody said she was the most disagreeable-looking child ever seen. It was true, too. She had a little thin face and a little thin body, thin light hair and a sour expression."[8] The first thing we see her doing is beating and kicking a native servant, and when she learns that her nurse has died she does not cry. "She was not an affectionate child and had never cared much for anyone."[9]

Colin is portrayed as spoiled and selfish: "He could have anything he asked for and was never made to do anything he did not like to do,"[10] and he too tyrannizes over servants. " 'Everyone is obliged to do what pleases me,' he said indifferently. 'It makes me ill to be angry.' "[11] Yet eventually Mary and Colin, like the old earl of Dorincourt, are converted to goodness and generosity. Also, like Cedric, they are restored to their natural birthright, which in this case is not temporal but spiritual; not money and position, but what Frances Hodgson Burnett considered the natural inheritance of mankind — love and joy.

One of the most innovative things about *The Secret Garden*, as Ann Thwaite remarks, is that the children are not reformed through the intervention of some wise and kind other person, but mainly through their own efforts, something very uncommon in earlier children's books. They do get some help from a local boy, Dickon, though only after they are well on their way.

And Mary and Colin are not just ordinary sulky or naughty children; they are severely neurotic. Today Mary, with her odd private games and cold indifference to her parents' deaths, might be diagnosed as preschizoid; bedridden Colin, with his imaginary hunchback, as a classic hysteric with conversion symptoms. Mrs. Burnett's presentation of their cases is astonishingly complete even by today's standards and plausibly grounded in the treatment both have received since birth. Mary has been almost totally neglected and unloved, while Colin's father has blamed him for his mother's death and consigned him to the care of servants and a doctor who stands to inherit the estate if Colin, already an invalid, should die.

The Secret Garden, like E. Nesbit's tales, presents ideas that could certainly be called subversive, since at the time they were new and of dubious reputation. In this case, however, they are ideas about religion, psychology, and health. Colin's self-hypnotic chanting recalls the sermons of Christian Science or New Thought, in both of which Mrs. Burnett was interested. The idea that illness is often largely psychological, and can be cured by positive thinking, permeates the book. Another new concept is that of the healing power of nature, of fresh air and outdoor exercise. Today we take ideas like this for granted, but Mrs. Burnett grew up in an age when the only exercise permitted to middle-class women was going for walks. *The Secret Garden* also shows the influence of the new paganism that found a following among liberal intellectuals of the time. It contains a kind of nature spirit in Dickon, the farm boy who spends whole days on the moors talking to plants and animals and who is a sort of cross between Kipling's Mowgli and the many adult incarnations of the rural Pan who appear in Edwardian fiction, rescuing E. M. Forster's heroines, and later D. H. Lawrence's, from death in life.

When it appeared, in 1911, *The Secret Garden* was only moderately successful — perhaps because it was ahead of its time, for since then its fame has grown steadily. In the 1970s, in fact, it seems to have become something of a cult book among high school and college students in America. And it isn't hard to see why, considering that *The Secret Garden* is the story of two unhappy, sickly, overcivilized children who achieve health and happiness through a combination of communal gardening, mystical faith, daily exercises, encounter-group-type confrontation, and a health-food diet.

America has changed a great deal since the sixties and seventies. Yet the underlying message of Mrs. Burnett's masterpiece, that one can save oneself with the help of friends, still has its — by now more subversive — appeal. Even in these conservative times it remains the most popular book in my college course in children's literature.

12

Back to Pooh Corner

A. A. MILNE

Help me if you can, I've got to get
Back to the House at Pooh Corner

. . . .

Back to the days of Christopher Robin and Pooh.[1]

I was surprised, some years ago, when I heard these words
sung to the accompaniment of electronic instruments and in
the same week saw on the back cover of *Rolling Stone* an
advertisement for another rock group, called Edward Bear.
But inquiry among my students confirmed it — Pooh was still
a big culture hero. He meant as much to the Now Generation
as he did to us Back When.

We not only read Milne's books over and over as children; all through high school and college we went on speaking
his language, seeing people and events in his terms. My
former husband lived his first term at prep school as Piglet,
with friends who were Pooh and Eeyore, and the school
grounds and surrounding country were remapped accord-
ingly. At college I knew girls who went by the names of
Tigger and Roo, and their counterparts can be found today
on many campuses.

But it is not only American students who remain Pooh fans. Millions of copies of Milne's books have been published in more than eighteen languages, including Serbo-Croatian and Esperanto; the Russian edition and the Latin *Winnie Ille Pooh* are used as texts in language courses. Pooh toys, calendars, T-shirts, and crockery are widely available. A Pooh workout book has recently appeared, as well as an introduction to Chinese philosophy by Benjamin Hoff entitled *The Tao of Pooh.*

Why should these mild tales about a group of English toys have almost instantly become, and remained for more than sixty years, international classics — probably the best-loved children's books of the twentieth century? Perhaps it is because, in spite of their apparent simplicity, *Winnie-the-Pooh* (1926) and its sequel, *The House at Pooh Corner* (1928), tell a story with universal appeal to anyone anywhere who finds himself, like most children, at a social disadvantage. What Milne has done is to turn the child's world upside down, creating a particularly elegant reversal of parental authority. In reality Christopher Robin is a very small boy in a world of adults; but in the Pooh books he rules over — and in the illustrations physically towers over — a society of smaller beings. He is the responsible adult, while those around him are merely animals or his old toys. (It is a delightful and literal working out of the last chapter of *Through the Looking-Glass,* when Alice discovers that the Red Queen, that frightening governess figure, is only her kitten.) Surely part of the universal appeal of the Pooh books is due to the pleasure any child must feel in imagining himself or herself larger, wiser, and more powerful than the surrounding adults.

READING THE Pooh books is easy and agreeable. Writing about them, on the other hand, has been awkward (if not impossible) since 1963, when Frederick C. Crews published *The Pooh Perplex*. It is not often that a satirical work achieves such success that it effectively destroys its object, but Crews almost managed it. Although he was not able to laugh into silence any of the dozen varieties of current literary criticism he so brilliantly parodied, he did manage to stifle almost all critical comment on Winnie-the-Pooh for a decade.[2] No one likes to imitate an imitation, and anyhow Crews had said most of what could be said about Pooh in one disguise or another; his best insights occur in the essay by "Harvey C. Window," which appears to be self-parody. Even now, I begin this piece with some embarrassment, aware that I am in part only following one of the suggestions for further "responsible criticism" made by Crews's "Smedley Force," a prominent member of the Modern Language Association who was "struck by the paucity of biographical connections between Winnie-the-Pooh and . . . A. A. Milne."[3]

At first glance, Milne appears to be writing about his son, Christopher Robin, who was six when *Winnie-the-Pooh* appeared, and about his son's toys. But there are indications that Milne was also thinking of his own childhood. For one thing, the setting of the books seems to suggest pre-1900 Essex and Kent, where Milne spent his holidays as a child, rather than the milder and more thickly settled countryside of Sussex, where he lived as an adult. The landscape is fairly bare and uncultivated, consisting mostly of heath and woods and marsh. There are many pine trees, and the most common plants seem to be gorse and thistles. Rain, wind, fog, and even snow are common.

Born in 1882, Alan Alexander Milne was the youngest of the three sons of John Vine Milne, the headmaster of a small suburban London school for boys. At Henley House the Milne children lived a half-private, half-public life, playing and eating with their father's pupils and joining the classes as soon as they were old enough. The world of Pooh repeats this situation in many respects. It is a small, old-fashioned, self-contained universe, without economic competition or professional ambition. There are no cars, planes, radios, or telephones; war, crime, and serious violence are unknown. Aggression is limited to the mildest form of practical joke, and even that generally backfires. Except for Kanga and Roo, there are no family relationships.

Pooh, like a schoolboy, lives in a society of eccentric but loyal friends, in which the main occupations are eating, exploration, visiting, and sports. Drama and excitement center on the capture of strange animals or the rescue of friends in danger, but the danger is always from natural causes — accidents, floods, storms. Apart from occasional bad weather, it is a perfectly safe world.

Milne claims in his *Autobiography* that he did not invent most of the characters in the Pooh books, but merely took over the toys that Christopher Robin happened to possess: "Their owner by constant affection had given them the twist in their features which denoted character. . . . They were what they are for anyone to see; I described rather than invented them. Only Rabbit and Owl were my own unaided work."[4]

Nevertheless, there seem to be some echoes from Milne's own past in the dramatis personae. Milne's father, whom he describes in his *Autobiography* as "the best man I have ever known,"[5] was a serious, kindly schoolmaster, devoted to all his sons, as well as to the boys whose temporary guardian he was. Yet everyone recognized that Alan was his favorite child. A similar situation occurs in the books, where Winnie-the-Pooh is the undisputed favorite of Christopher Robin. As a child Milne believed that his father "knew everything there was to know"; but in fact he was pedantic rather than wise. ("Later on . . . I formed the opinion that, even if Father knew everything, he knew most of it wrong."[6]) In this aspect Milne senior may appear as Owl, the pompous schoolmaster ("If anyone knows anything about anything, . . . it's Owl who knows something about something"[7]) who turns out to be nearly illiterate, unable even to spell his own name.

Milne's happy childhood centered on his father. As for his mother, he remarks: "I don't think I ever really knew her. When I was a child I neither experienced, nor felt the need of, that mother-love of which one reads so much . . . I gave my heart to my father."[8]

He remembers his mother chiefly as a sensible, very efficient housekeeper ("She could do everything better than the people whom so reluctantly she came to employ: cook better than the cook, dust better than the parlour-maid"[9]). Like Rabbit in the Pooh books, she lived in a state of preoccupation with small responsibilities and bossy concern for the duties of others. It is interesting that Rabbit, the officious organizer, and Owl, the solemn pedant — the characters most like caricatures of Milne's own parents — are also the only ones he claims to have invented himself, the live animals among the toys.

Next to his father, Milne's greatest attachment as a child was to his brother Ken, sixteen months older. Ken, he writes, was "kinder, larger-hearted, more lovable, more tolerant";[10] but Alan was brighter and quicker, though more timid. Like Pooh and Piglet, they were inseparable, so much so that they had hardly any use for other people: "We had two day-dreams. The first was of a life on the sea. . . . Our other dream . . . was, quite simply, that we should wake up one morning and find that everybody else in the world was dead."[11] Or, as Pooh puts it:

I could spend a happy morning
  Seeing Piglet
And I couldn't spend a happy morning
  Not seeing Piglet
And it doesn't seem to matter
If I don't see Owl or Eeyore (or any of the others)
And I'm not going to see Owl or Eeyore (or any of the
  others)[12]

Some of these others may also have real-life prototypes, either in Milne's childhood or that of his son. There is Kanga, the kind, fussy mother or nanny, with her continual "We'll see, dear" and lack of interest in anything except children and counting "how many pieces of soap there were left, and the two clean spots in Tigger's feeder."[13] Bouncy Tigger and little Roo are like many younger siblings, always pushing themselves forward in a noisy, simpleminded way, but of no use in serious matters. Their arrival in the Forest, like the appearance of a younger brother or sister in early childhood, is sudden and unexplained: "Here — we — are — . . . And then, suddenly, we wake up one morning, and what do we find? We find a Strange Animal among us. An animal of whom we had never even heard before!"[14] Rabbit, Pooh, and Piglet form a plot to get rid of Roo, but as might be expected, it fails — like Tigger in the sequel, he must be accepted into the Forest.

Finally there is Eeyore, the complete pessimist ("I shouldn't be surprised if it hailed a good deal tomorrow"[15]), who is depressive with delusions of persecution where Tigger is manic with delusions of grandeur. ("Somebody must have taken it," he remarks when his tail is lost. "How Like Them."[16]) Eeyore may date from a later period in Milne's life, the years 1906–14, when he worked on *Punch*. The editor at that time was Owen Seaman, "a strange, unlucky man,"[17] according to Milne, always dissatisfied and suspicious, and given to blaming his errors on extraneous circumstances. Upon losing a golf match, Milne relates, Seaman "threw down his putter and said 'That settles it. I'll never play in knickerbockers again.' "[18]

THOUGH THE characters in *Winnie-the-Pooh* were drawn from Milne's own life and that of his son, they are also figures who might appear in any childhood. Who has not had a cheerfully reckless friend like Tigger, or a wryly gloomy one like Eeyore? Even more to the point, what child — or adult — has not had days when he or she felt like Tigger or like Eeyore, or as small and nervous as Piglet? It was Milne's genius to have created, working from such apparently simple materials, these universal types, and to have constructed in a few acres of English countryside a world that has the qualities both of the Golden Age of history and legend, and the lost paradise of childhood — two eras that, according to psychologists, are often one in the unconscious mind.

Among the characters seen from a child's viewpoint, Pooh is the child himself. The rest have virtues and faults particular to some adults and some children; Pooh, the hero, has the virtues and faults common to all children. He is simple, natural, and affectionate. But he is also a Bear of Very Little Brain, continually falling into ludicrous errors of judgment and comprehension — he is so greedy that he eats Eeyore's birthday jar of honey on his way to deliver it. Yet these faults are also endearing; all of us at birth were stupid and greedy, but no less lovable for that. As Milne himself has remarked, children combine natural innocence and grace with a "brutal egotism."[19]

"Oh, Bear!" said Christopher Robin. "How I do love you!"

"So do I," said Pooh.[20]

But slow though he is, Pooh always comes through in an emergency. When Roo falls into the river, everyone behaves in a typical way:

> "Look at me swimming," squeaked Roo from the middle of his pool, and was hurried down a waterfall into the next pool.
>
> Everybody was doing something to help. Piglet . . . was jumping up and down and making "Oo, I say" noises; Owl was explaining that in a case of Sudden and Temporary Immersion the Important Thing was to keep the Head Above Water; Kanga was jumping along the bank, saying "Are you *sure* you're all right, Roo dear?" . . . Eeyore had turned round and hung his tail over the first pool into which Roo fell, and with his back to the accident was grumbling quietly to himself. . . .
>
> "Get something across the stream lower down, some of you fellows," called Rabbit.[21]

But it is Pooh who rescues Roo, just as he later rescues Piglet; it is Pooh who discovers the "North Pole."

If Pooh is the child as hero, Christopher Robin is the child as God. He is also the ideal parent. He is both creator and judge — the two divine functions shared by mortal parents. He does not participate in most of the adventures but usually appears at the end of the chapter, sometimes descending with a machine (an umbrella, a popgun, et cetera) to save the situation.

Milne's ironic view of the adult world and its pretensions is sometimes undercut by another sort of irony addressed to adults who might be reading the book aloud. These passages, which appear mostly at the beginning of *Winnie-the-Pooh* (there are none in the sequel), take the form of condescending conversations between the author and Christopher Robin.

> "Was that me?" said Christopher Robin in an awed voice, hardly daring to believe it.
>
> "That was you."
>
> Christopher Robin said nothing, but his eyes got larger and larger, and his face got pinker and pinker.[22]

Behind the godlike child is another and more powerful deity: A. A. Milne, who has created both Christopher Robin and Pooh.

There are other partly concealed messages from the author to the adult or adolescent reader. The verbal hypocrisies of greed are mocked in Tigger, those of cowardice in Piglet, and those of polite etiquette in Rabbit. A similar criticism may lie behind the frequent attempts of the characters to elaborate some error or misunderstanding into a system, as with Pooh and Piglet's hunt for the Woozle. As soon as a real fact or observation is introduced, the system collapses, and the Woozle vanishes.

Milne's language, too, contains hidden messages. He pretends not to understand long words and makes fun of people who use them. He employs a special form of punctuation, capitalizing words usually written with a lowercase letter, as is done now only in theatrical and film publicity. But in the Pooh books the effect is reversed: Milne capitalizes to show that though the character takes something seriously, the reader need not do so. When Pooh remarks "I have been Foolish and Deluded,"[23] the words are weakened by the capital letters; to have said that Pooh was foolish and deluded would have been much stronger.

A subversive side effect of this procedure is to weaken

words that are conventionally capitalized and, by extension, the things they stand for. Milne was aware of this; in an essay on his poem "The King's Breakfast" he makes a suggestion for reading aloud the lines:

> The King asked
> The Queen and
> The Queen asked
> The Dairymaid

> Don't be afraid of saying "and" at the end of the second line; the second and third words have the same value, and you need not be alarmed because one is a royal noun and the other is only a common conjunction.[24]

When Milne uses a word, it means what he tells it to mean; his Bears and Expeditions are of a very special kind. He makes the rules; he determines what things and emotions will be allowed into his books and on what terms.

In the same way, when Milne came to write his *Autobiography* he tended to remember selectively. His own childhood appears through a kind of golden haze: "The sun is shining, goodness and mercy are to follow me (it seems) for ever, . . . fifty years from now I shall still dream at times that I am walking up Priory Road."[25]

As Milne himself once announced, "art is not life, but an exaggeration of it; life reinforced by the personality of the artist."[26] And an exaggerated, sentimental — and also sometimes rather condescending — tone appears at times in the *Autobiography*, especially when Milne speaks of his father. Describing his own departure for boarding school, he writes:

> Farewell, Papa, with your brave, shy heart and your funny little ways; with your humour and your wisdom and your never-failing goodness; . . . "Well," you will tell yourself, "it lasted until he was twelve; they grow

up and resent our care for them, they form their own
ideas, and think ours old-fashioned. It is natural. But
oh, to have that little boy again, whom I used to throw
up to the sky, his face laughing down into mine — "[27]

This nostalgic theme recurs in the Pooh books, particularly in the final chapter of *The House at Pooh Corner:*

"Pooh, when I'm — *you* know . . . will you come up
here sometimes?"
"Just Me?"
"Yes, Pooh."
"Will you be here too?"
"Yes, Pooh, I will be, really. I *promise* I will be, Pooh."
"That's good," said Pooh.[28]

This is also sentimentality, but a sentimentality that
rises into pathos, by means of the pathetic fallacy. In fact,
the world of childhood and the past, our discarded toys and
landscapes, will not mourn us when we leave; the regret will
be felt by our own imprisoned earlier selves. Milne ascribes
to his father and to Pooh the passionate regret he feels for
his own lost paradise.

Winnie-the-Pooh is essentially a modern version of an
archetypal legend. It is a very old one (almost the first, in
biblical terms) — the story of a peaceful animal kingdom ruled
by a single benevolent human being. Milne even tells us that
Christopher Robin, like Adam, gave names to his subjects.

It seems no accident, therefore, that the threat of
change and loss enters this Eden in the shape of a tree of
knowledge. One day, Christopher Robin is discovered to be
missing from the Forest. He has gone to school for the first
time and is learning his alphabet, beginning with the letter *A*.
Piglet comes across this letter *A*, arranged on the ground
out of three sticks, and thinks "that perhaps it was a Trap

of some kind."[29] Eeyore, a little later, is first respectful and then contemptuous: " 'Clever!' said Eeyore scornfully, putting a foot heavily on his three sticks. 'Education!' said Eeyore bitterly, jumping on his six sticks. 'What *is* Learning? . . . A thing *Rabbit* knows!' "[30]

He is right to be bitter. It is Education that will, by the end of *The House at Pooh Corner,* have driven Christopher Robin out of his self-created Eden.

No wonder that this particular lost paradise, this small, safe, happy place where individuality and privacy are respected, should appeal to people growing up into a world of telegrams, anger, wiretapping, war, death, and taxes — especially to those. who would rather not grow up. Milne's loosely organized society of unemployed artists and eccentrics, each quietly doing his own thing, might have a special attraction for counterculture types. For them, Pooh Corner would be both the lost past and the ideal future — at once the golden rural childhood they probably never knew, and the perfect commune they are always seeking.

13

Heroes for Our Time

J. R. R. TOLKIEN AND

T. H. WHITE

In all countries at all times there are official Pollyanna versions of national history and current events. Ours is a Great Nation with a Great Tradition; life here has never been better; and if we have problems, they are being valiantly overcome. Nowhere is the official version more loudly advertised than in school textbooks, where hints that all is not well, or perhaps was not well in the past, kindle a fire storm of abuse from parents and government officials. Low-circulation journals may expose the shaky condition of the ship of state, the holes in the hull and the rats sloshing about down below, but God forbid that our children should hear of them too soon.

But children, innocent though they may be, are quick to pick up clues to social and historical truth. Besides, they have help. For years, some of the most gifted writers of fiction and fantasy have portrayed, though often in disguised form, the realities of the past and the current political situation.

A century ago, for instance, when half the globe was colored red, the heroes of English adventure stories escaped from savages, rescued captives, and discovered treasure all round the world. Under the direction of R. M. Ballantyne, Robert Louis Stevenson, and Rudyard Kipling, they traveled to Alaska and Africa and Asia; they met holy men in India and outwitted pirates in the South Seas. But as the sun wearily set on the British Empire, fictional heroism began to be located nearer home, where there was still enough light to see by.

Kipling, more sensitive to historical currents than he is sometimes thought, was one of the first authors to make the shift. *Puck of Pook's Hill* (1906), like his earlier tales, celebrates the greatness of Britain and the sterling character of Englishmen. But now this greatness is displayed not in colonial parts, but in the English past. Puck, that most British of fairies, takes the children Una and Dan back into time to observe the exemplary behavior of Englishmen (and an occasional Englishwoman) during the Roman period, after the Norman Conquest, in the Elizabethan Age, and so on. The preeminence of the nation, he suggests, is a matter of luck and geography rather than heroism, and our best course is to admire and emulate the traditional British virtues of ironic humor, modest courage, and the stiff upper lip.

Thirty years later, when the empire had shrunk still further, two other gifted writers followed Kipling's lead. J.R.R. Tolkien seemed to have drawn his material from the medieval sagas, with their noisy battles between men and monsters and their simple social and moral structure. But the message of *The Hobbit* (1937) was new. It presented a world in which the forces of evil might at times overcome the forces of good, and the true hero was no longer strong, handsome, aristocratic, and victorious in combat.

As many commentators have pointed out, the political geography of Tolkien's Middle-earth suggests a map of Western Europe in the 1930s. In the upper left-hand corner of the map is the Shire, a peaceful region of farms and villages that resembles rural England. The farther east you go, the more dangerous and unsettled conditions become, and the lower right-hand side — about where Germany and Italy would be — is a region of horror and desolation.*

Bilbo, the hero of *The Hobbit,* is a most unlikely hero from the official point of view. He is an ordinary, unambitious little person who is forced into adventure rather than going to look for it. At the start of his quest for the dragon's treasure he is called a burglar rather than a treasure-hunter — perhaps suggesting that adventures seem like crimes to respectable people. Perhaps Tolkien is also saying, in a quiet way, that property is theft. In the course of the book Bilbo's indifference to glory in battle and to great wealth turns out to be a valuable quality; it takes a very long time for power to corrupt him. Several critics have seen in Bilbo's reluctant but steadfast efforts a foreshadowing of the courage and endurance of British citizens in World War II. Others have remarked that Bilbo's journey from respectable dullness to the position of an outsider with wonderful memories who is no longer considered respectable by his neighbors has something in common with Tolkien's own life history. While he was simply an Oxford philologist he enjoyed the esteem of his fellow academics; after he began to publish fantasies for children he was no longer considered quite serious or grown up.

But if he lost the confidence of his colleagues, Tolkien was amply rewarded. Today his books are classics. A new annotated edition of *The Hobbit* has recently appeared, and today the sun never sets on readers of *The Lord of the Rings,* while the legend FRODO LIVES is sighted on the walls of Ca-

---

*It is only fair to say that Tolkien consistently denied that there was any allegorical or topical meaning to his work. But though he may not be responsible for what readers have made of it, he certainly provided them with material.

nadian college buildings, Australian bridges, and New York subway stations.

TOLKIEN, in inventing his imaginary world, turned to Norse myth and medieval legend. His contemporary T. H. White chose to place his tale in the later, sadder, and wiser period of Sir Thomas Malory's Arthurian chronicles. White's brilliant four-volume novel, *The Once and Future King,* is both an amusing tale of magic and adventure for children and a sophisticated tragedy for adults; a celebration of an ideal past England and a lament for the contemporary one.

Though White was at least as good a writer as Tolkien, his work is much more uneven, and its reception has been equally so. The tetralogy's first volume, *The Sword in the Stone,* was an instant success when it appeared in 1938; but though the later books had been completed (and two of them issued separately) by 1941, White's London publisher declined to print them together, as he had previously agreed to do. The dispute centered on a final, fifth volume, *The Book of Merlyn,* in which King Arthur, defeated on the battlefield and with his Round Table in ruins, considers the problem of man's innate destructiveness. Moreover, White had revised the earlier volumes in line with this theme. The new pacifist slant of the book was not well received by White's editor, who pleaded that wartime paper shortages now prevented his issuing it.

Long and often disagreeable negotiations and revisions followed, and *The Once and Future King* did not appear until 1958 — and then it was minus its original conclusion.[1] Though the book was a tremendous success both in England and America, it took nearly another twenty years for the final volume to be published as White had written it. If he had lived, he would not have been surprised; he expected this sort of treatment from the world.

Terence Hanbury White, like Kipling, was born in India of British parents and, also like Kipling, was forcibly uprooted from his childhood environment at the age of five and sent home to England. But, unlike Kipling, he was unlucky in his parents. He had what his biographer Sylvia Townsend Warner has called "a menacing psychopathic mother"[2] who alternately demanded his love and rejected it. As he wrote later: "Either there were the dreadful parental quarrels and spankings . . . or there were excessive scenes of affection during which she wooed me to love her — not her to love me. . . . anyway, she managed to bitch up my loving women."[3] In England he was sent to a series of classically bad boarding schools where the beatings he had received from his parents continued.

White grew up to be a complex and haunted man, both sensitively poetic and athletically gung ho, whose best work was written for, or at least originally intended for, children. If he were himself the hero of a tale of magic, he would have been one of those princes whose christenings are attended not only by the usual twelve good fairies but by an equal number of malevolent ones. He was large, handsome, courageous, witty, imaginative, and industrious; he was well born and well educated, a fine athlete and sportsman, intellectually gifted (he gained a First with Distinction from Cambridge) and a natural writer, with one of the best prose styles of his generation. He was also alcoholic, homosexual, and subject to severe depressions and obsessive fears of failure and public rejection.

White grew up not only unable to love women but, by his own choice, cut off from intimacy even with the men he might have loved. As David Garnett, in whom he confided, reports it: "[He] explained to me that he was a sadist and that his imagination was frequently occupied with sadistic fantasies. He explained also that this had been disastrous whenever he was passionately in love. . . . In love he was always in a dilemma: if he behaved with sincerity, and instinctively, he alienated his lover and horrified and disgusted himself."[4]

Several years of psychoanalysis, though they helped to reconcile White to his condition, did nothing to change it. During most of his adult life, his only happy emotional attachments were to birds and animals: the falcons he flew for sport, the owls he kept as pets, above all a red setter bitch named Brownie who meant as much to White as My Dog Tulip did to J. R. Ackerley, and whose death left him half-crazed and utterly desolate. ("I died last night. All that me is dead, because it was half her." "She was wife, mother, mistress & child. . . . I am so lonely and can't stop crying and it is the shock."[5]) After Brownie was buried, White went to Dublin "and kept myself as drunk as possible for nine days."[6]

Even apart from his sexual problems, White was handicapped by his inability to be close to other people. ("I have no friends, only acquaintances. You have no idea how curious it is to live one's whole life like a cat."[7]) He had a self-confessed "sense of inferiority . . . of danger . . . of disaster"[8] and a Hemingway-like compulsion to test himself physically, which led him to fly small planes, jump dangerous horses, drive much too fast, and descend into the sea in a diving suit — always in a state of mingled fear and exhilaration. It is surprising that White had only one serious accident: he drove his Bentley through a cottage wall and right into the bedroom where an elderly couple was sleeping.

The Sword in the Stone was written during one of the happiest periods of White's life, in the autumn of 1937. He had made enough from a series of spy thrillers to quit teaching boarding school and move into a cottage in Buckinghamshire with his dog Brownie and three hawks. The book was conceived as a kind of prologue to Malory, describing the boyhood of the future King Arthur. "The Wart," as he is known, lives as a poor relation in the castle of his guardian, Sir Ector, bullied and condescended to by Sir Ector's son Kay. Merlyn, who becomes the boys' tutor, magically transforms the Wart into various birds and beasts and sends him among them to learn the wisdom, courage, and virtue necessary for a future king. It is a fine story, full of energy and comic invention and detailed information about life in fifteenth-century England.

The Book of Merlyn was composed in the winter of 1940–41, while White was self-exiled in rural Ireland, cut off from his country and the war in which most of his friends were engaged. His pacifist views, and his guilt about avoiding responsibility and fear that he was in fact a coward, combined to make him completely miserable. It may seem odd to some that a self-confessed sadist should also be a pacifist. But it should be remembered that White was revolted by his own sadism; and war, for such a person, must seem doubly horrible, because it allows the acting out or at least witnessing of forbidden fantasies. It is also terrifying because of the possibility that one may be the victim rather than the perpetrator of deliberate cruelty. Like many people who believe their deepest impulses to be evil, White extended this belief to others, with the result that, as Sylvia Townsend Warner writes, "he was basically afraid of the human race."[9]

In his journal White went over and over the implications of the possible courses open to him: "to be a conscientious objector, and then to fight, and then to seek some constructive wartime employment which might combine creative work with service to my country. All these sad and terrified dashes from one hunted corner to the next."[10]

This state of mind and these obsessive arguments leaked into the book he was writing, interrupting the story and almost destroying what might have been a brilliant conclusion to his most ambitious work. "I have suddenly discovered," he wrote to his former tutor at Cambridge, "that (1) the central theme of Morte d'Arthur is to find an antidote to war, (2) that the best way to examine the politics of man is to observe him, with Aristotle, as a political animal."[11]

If White had followed this plan from the start he might have written a better book; but instead he begins *The Book of Merlyn* by setting up an underground seminar in which Merlyn, Arthur, and all the animals from *The Sword in the Stone* (Archimedes the owl, the badger, the hedgehog, and the rest) discuss patterns of aggression among men and other species. Like all seminars, it is composed in equal parts of pedantry, humor, interesting questions, stupid answers, amusing digressions, repetition, and boredom.

The book improves a great deal when the lesson turns from tell to show, and Arthur, for the last time, is transformed by his old tutor, Merlyn. First, as a red ant, he enters a disagreeable totalitarian community, which goes into war with a twenty-four-hour blast of radio propaganda ("Antland, Antland Over All") and specious political logic:

> A. We are more numerous than they are, therefore we have a right to their syrup.
>
> B. They are more numerous than we are, therefore they are wickedly trying to steal our syrup. . . .
>
> G. If we do not attack them today, they will attack us tomorrow.
>
> H. In any case we are not attacking them at all: we are offering them incalculable benefits.[12]

But White's description of Antland is directed not only at fascist and communist regimes, but also at contemporary Britain, of which he wrote in his journal:

> There don't seem to be many people being killed yet — no hideous slaughters of gas and bacteria.

But the truth is going.

We are suffocating in propaganda instead of gas, slowly feeling our minds go dead.

And on the wireless — it seems as if it must be hundreds of millions of times a day — the foulest and cheapest and vulgarest and most debasing. They sing or play nothing but "We'll hang out the washing on the Siegfried line" or "Run, Adolf, run, Adolf, run, run, run." . . . Devils in hell must sing like this.[13]

After a mercifully brief return to the underground seminar, Arthur is sent into a world as superior to the human one as that of the ants is inferior. He becomes a wild goose on the marshes of East Anglia. These chapters are as good as anything White ever wrote — but they were not originally written in these dark months. Rather, they are the remains of an unfinished novel, *Grief for the Grey Goose,* begun in 1938, before England was at war and White in exile. The geese are social, yet solitary; as noble and beautiful and strong, as affectionate and innocent, as Jonathan Swift's Houyhnhnms; and their journey across the North Sea is wonderfully described:

Sometimes, when they came down from the cirrus levels to catch a better wind, they would find themselves among the flocks of cumulus: huge towers of modelled vapour, looking as white as Monday's washing and as solid as meringues. Perhaps one of these piled-up blossoms of the sky, these snow-white droppings of a gigantic Pegasus, would lie before them several miles away. They would set their course towards it, seeing it grow bigger silently and imperceptibly, a motionless growth; and then, when they were at it, . . . the sun would dim. Wraiths of mist suddenly moving like serpents of the air would coil about them for a second.

Grey damp would be around them, and the sun, a copper penny, would fade away.[14]

When Arthur is snatched back out of this world by Merlyn he is overcome with regret and bitterness, like Gulliver, and refuses to have anything more to do with mankind. However, he is persuaded to take a final look at his country; and as he sits on a hill gazing over England, he is moved; his resolve weakens; he realizes that England is his responsibility and "that peace was more important than a kingdom."[15] He returns to his own world and almost succeeds in making a treaty with his enemies and ending the war. But at the last moment, when the opposing armies are drawn up on the battlefield to sign the truce, everything goes wrong. A snake moves in the grass (perhaps symbolically), a soldier draws his sword to strike at it, the other side suspects treachery, and the fighting begins again.

But even this is not the end. Everyone knows, White says, that the Round Table is broken and its knights scattered; but about Arthur himself we are not quite sure. Many believe that he is not dead but only sleeping, and will come again. And the persistence of this belief, and of the legend of King Arthur and his knights, is hopeful in itself; though, as Merlyn says, "nobody can be saved from anything, unless they save themselves."[16]

White is less dogmatic than some present-day sociobiologists. He does not claim that because other species are mindless totalitarians, or noble anarchists, a natural disposition toward totalitarianism or anarchy persists in the lower levels of the human brain. His estimate of our prospects is deeply pessimistic, but not fatalistic; that is, it offers neither the comfort of optimism nor the comfort of despair. Peace on earth is always possible and desirable, if very unlikely.

It is not surprising that *The Book of Merlyn* was received

unenthusiastically by a London publisher in 1941. Anyone who lived through that period will remember how, in both Britain and America, an unquestioning patriotism and optimism was the only possible public attitude; anything else was considered not only subversive but almost wicked.

What seems odder, though certainly characteristic of White's life, is the postwar fate of his chronicles of King Arthur. Again, the good and bad fairies were at work, some arranging for *The Once and Future King* to become famous throughout the world as a Broadway musical and Hollywood film, others making sure that *Camelot* would be a glossy travesty, sentimental and pretty where the book was skeptical and passionate. It is quite appropriate that John F. Kennedy's court, often at the time of his reign compared to the musical and film versions of Camelot, turned out in the end to have been a lot more like White's chronicle, with its flawed heroes, its inspiring public rhetoric and scandalous private revelations — and, of course, its awful end.

The power of a stage or film adaptation to destroy its original ("No, but I saw the movie, and it was lousy") is tremendous, and no doubt *Camelot* is partly responsible for the relative obscurity into which White's work has now fallen, especially in relation to that of his near-contemporary Tolkien. But there are other, more basic factors involved.

TOLKIEN'S books have two messages. The first is that the ordinary small man (hobbits are literally small, under five feet) can play an essential and heroic part in the defeat of evil. Bilbo and Frodo succeed not through superior skill or strength or wisdom but, like the heroes of the old folktales, by the exercise of the small-town, middle-class virtues of simplicity, good nature, ingenuity, and patient determination. The knights of the Round Table, by contrast, are highly trained jock aristocrats, much more difficult for the contemporary

reader — the average American college freshman, for instance — to identify with.

Tolkien's second message is that evil must be tolerated
because good may somehow come of it, as when the repulsive
Gollum bites off Frodo's finger in order to obtain the magic
ring and then falls with it into a volcano, thus destroying both
himself and the evil power of the ring. This is an impressive
and satisfying scene, but the principle involved, if applied to
some real-life situation (such as the presence of Gollum-like
officials in high places) seems rather dangerous. White, on
the other hand, had no confidence that good would come out
of evil — or even out of good.

In spite of the wonderful richness of his fantasy, Tolkien's moral imagination is essentially simple. Good and evil
for him are distinct and separate: his heroes have only lovable
(often comically lovable) defects, and his villains lack all agreeable traits. At the most, we feel a sort of distant pity for
them. White, unfortunately for the success of his books, saw
things in a more complex way. The noblest characters in his
work are flawed: Arthur by credulity and fits of weak despair,
Lancelot by self-hatred and the inability to resist sexual passion even at the price of betrayal and dishonor. Moreover,
many of White's worst characters have redeeming, even lik-
able qualities.

The Lord of the Rings is a fantasy in more ways than
one. It portrays an unreal world in which serious wickedness
is exterior not only psychologically but geographically. Crime
in Hobbiton-over-the-water is limited to occasional public
squabbling and petty thievery; to find your opponent, you
must go on a long journey.

The first book of White's tetralogy, *The Sword in the
Stone*, is subversive without being hopeless. The Wart, the
shabby little boy who begins as the teased and scorned foster
child of Sir Ector, becomes King Arthur, in the process en-

joying many adventures, some of which take him into strangely twentieth-century surroundings, including an ice cream parlor with jazz music. (For a child reader, the deliberate anachronisms are part of the subversive fun.)

But in the final version of *The Once and Future King*, and in *The Book of Merlyn*, the situation has become more serious. Evil and danger are located not in a distant part of the map beyond the Misty Mountains, as in Tolkien; they are right there at home; and if you want to see your enemy's face, just look in the mirror. No wonder adult readers prefer Tolkien: nobody likes bad news, especially when it might be true.

14

The Power of Smokey

RICHARD ADAMS

Today, it has been suggested to me, anything goes in fiction; there is no need for "subversive" literature, either adult or juvenile. Such statements are made in every age: if you are part of the picture it is always difficult to see what has been left out or hidden. That is why we need writers, to discover and reveal such secrets, often in a form that deliberately disguises their revelations. After a little time has passed the picture becomes clear, and we can see what has happened.

Richard Adams's most successful fantasy, *Watership Down* (1972), was ostensibly an animal story. After being rejected by most of the major publishing houses in Britain, it was issued by a small firm and became an overnight success. Eventually it was read by more than a million people and declared a modern classic.

"That rabbit book," as it was usually known — even today hardly anyone I know can remember the title, which suggests a sinking boat — became an international bestseller not only because it was well written and original. It was attractive also because it put forward political ideas and celebrated qualities many serious novelists were then afraid or embarrassed to write about.

In the early seventies, when characters were presented

as admirable it was usually because of their individual eccentricity and their independence of conventional values and the ties of family and society. The heroes and heroines of most serious novels were sad, bumbling failures; hysterical combatants in the sex war; or self-deceptive men and women of ill will. In *Watership Down,* on the other hand, one could read of characters who had honor and courage and dignity, who would risk their lives for others, whose love for their families and friends and community was enduring and effective — even if they looked like Flopsy, Mopsy, and Benjamin Bunny.

The book also, though published in a radical period and an expanding economy, has a conservative ecological message. It relates the adventures of a tribe of British rabbits who must flee their warren in the Berkshires when it is bulldozed flat for a construction site. Richard Adams was for many years an air-pollution expert with the British Department of the Environment; he saw what was happening to the British landscape long before many of his contemporaries did, and his portrait of the process is devastating. He was also a gifted naturalist, able to portray the daily life of his characters in accurate and fascinating detail.[1]

At the same time *Watership Down,* like George Orwell's *Animal Farm,* is a political fable. In the course of the story, the rabbit heroes meet and reject — or escape from — other rabbits who represent laid-back laissez-faire hedonism (a more immediate danger at the time the book was published) and planned-economy authoritarianism.

With *Shardik* (1974), a six-hundred-page novel about some imaginary barbarians who worship an imaginary bear, Richard Adams was attempting something more difficult, and — possibly as a result — his new book did not receive the welcome given its predecessor. Perhaps in *Shardik* Adams had not disguised his political message sufficiently. In spite of its title and the picture on the jacket, the book is not about a tribe of bears, though as before Adams's knowledge of the habits of the species is profound. Essentially, *Shardik* is about men, some of whom are just as sympathetic and admirable as the heroes of *Watership Down*.

This time, instead of setting his tale in a known time and place, Adams invented an imaginary primitive world: the ancient Beklan Empire, complete with history, geography, climate, culture, and religion. When the story begins, Bekla is in the hands of conquerors, and its former rulers, the Ortelgans, survive only as primitive island hunters who worship God in the form of a giant bear.

Bears, of course, have always been very popular in English literature, though — or perhaps because — they are unknown in English life outside of zoos. From the comic butts of the fables and the enchanted princes of folklore, through Kipling's wise, paternal Baloo, to Pooh and Paddington, they have always been portrayed as friendly; mischievous or clumsy sometimes, but easily domesticated and affectionate.

Richard Adams's Shardik, the Power of God, is a different sort of animal, more American than English. Like the eponymous hero of William Faulkner's story "The Bear," he is a figure of terror and mystery, violent and unpredictable. He is Nature, literally red in tooth and claw, both dangerous and beautiful, fearful and desirable. *Shardik*, like *Watership Down*, is among other things an ecological novel, an allegory and history of the relationship between human beings and the physical world. And here, too, Richard Adams shows his gift for descriptive prose. *Shardik* begins with a brilliant set piece on a forest fire:

> The wind strengthened, bringing a sound that seemed to stretch across the forest from end to end — a sound like a dry waterfall or the breathing of a giant. . . .

The sound grew to a roaring and the creatures flying before it became innumerable. Many were almost spent, yet still stumbled forward with open mouths set in snarls and staring eyes that saw nothing. Some tripped and were trampled down. Drifts of green smoke appeared through gaps in the undergrowth. . . . The heat increased until no living thing — not a lizard, not a fly — remained in the glade about the rock. . . . A single flame darted through the curtain of creepers, disappeared, returned and flickered in and out like a snake's tongue. A spray of dry, sharp-toothed leaves on a *zeltazla* bush caught fire and flared brightly, throwing a dismal shine on the smoke that was now filling the glade like fog. Immediately after, the whole wall of foliage at the top of the slope was ripped from the bottom as though by a knife of flame.[2]

Shardik's adventures parallel what has happened to the natural resources of the planet over time. On his first appearance, driven out of his native jungle by the fire and badly burned, he terrifies a half-savage Ortelgan hunter for whom nature is an overwhelming force to be dreaded and propitiated. Next, for a little while, the bear is healed and tended. Then gradually he is surrounded, captured, and imprisoned, though never really tamed. As he passes from the control of primitive people to that of a more sophisticated and urban civilization, Shardik is increasingly misused, neglected, and exploited under the pretense of being cared for and adored — just as our wilderness has often been destroyed under the guise of preservation. (Whenever we hear that some especially agreeable part of the local landscape is going to become a "recreation area," we know what it means: shadowy pine woods full of trailer hookups, mountain lakes echoing to the birdlike calls of outboard motors, and sunny meadows bright with rusted beer cans and broken glass.) And just as nature, too much abused, can turn against man, so eventually Shardik, dying, turns on his enemies and savages them.

Irritable reviewers, perhaps thinking of his first appearance in the book, have compared Shardik with Smokey the Bear; and in a sense he is what Smokey would be, taken seriously. Even Smokey has his Faulknerian side; he is not small and cuddly, but much larger than the cartoon people he usually confronts. He is generally represented as scowling, even threatening — and what, after all, does he intend to do with that shovel he carries, blade up?

But *Shardik* is not just an ecological allegory; the book can also be read as a study in the psychology of religion. It cannot be accidental that the central symbol chosen by Richard Adams, the survivor of a Jungian analysis, harks back to what anthropologists have called the oldest surviving evidence of mythological belief, discovered in the mountain caves inhabited by Neanderthal man before 50,000 B.C. There, ten thousand years earlier than the wall paintings of prehistoric hunters, the skulls of cave bears were grouped around a fire in the deepest rooms of the caves.

Shardik, like the cave bears, is not really a magical being; he is not anthropomorphized. All that he does is within the range of normal animal behavior, and only to those who believe in him does it seem symbolical, an act of God. Because of this belief, however, lives and societies are changed utterly; hundreds of men, women, and children die; a barbaric empire is destroyed and rebuilt and destroyed again, and finally brought a little nearer to civilized humanism.

One of Shardik's first effects is to set men against women: the Ortelgan warriors, who want the bear to lead them to victory over Bekla even if they have to drag him onto the battlefield in a cage, and the priestesses of the neighboring island, Quiso, who — like the bear-worshiping women and girls at the Temple of Brauron, in classical Greece — wish only to feed the bear, heal him, and sing to him. This part of the book should make some amends to feminists for the condescending treatment of the female rabbits — Flopsys and Mopsys all — in *Watership Down.* Through most of *Shardik,* women are not only important but more admirable generally and closer to nature and the truth than men are. Unfortunately, Adams does not carry this theme through, and the Good Society established in the happy ending is illogically and disappointingly patriarchal.

In the course of his book, Adams manages to picture most known Western varieties of religious attitude, from the simple totemistic faith of the Ortelgans through the Dionysiac intoxication of the young priestesses of Quiso to the obsessive ritualism or half-superstitious, half-conventional holiday observances of the rich Beklan townspeople, who light their torches at the annual Fire Festival in the spirit of an American parent plugging in the Christmas tree.

Agnosticism and atheism, both primitive and sophisticated, are not forgotten. The High Baron of Ortelga, when informed that Lord Shardik, the Power of God, has appeared on his island, reacts as most shrewd temporal (or spiritual) rulers would to a reputed miracle: by trying to suppress it and persuade the High Priestess to help him. His argument, though unsuccessful, is highly pragmatic:

> "We have found a large bear — possibly the largest bear that has ever lived. . . . But if you heal it, what will follow? . . . Even supposing that it does not kill you, at the best it will leave the island and then you, having tried to make use of it and failed, will lose influence over the people. . . . As a memory and a legend, Shardik has power and that power is ours, but to try to make

the people believe that he has returned can end in nothing but harm."[3]

The introduction of such characters has a secondary advantage: by overrepresenting the skeptical position, they parody and deflect the objections of a skeptical reader. This is especially true in the case of the aristocrat Elleroth, a sort of Gore Vidal figure, whose scorn of all religious faith is sure to outdo that of most readers:

> "You don't understand the dynamic ideas prevalent down on the river where the reeds all shiver. Matters there are determined by resort to hocus-pocus, mumbo jumbo and even, for all I know, jiggery-pokery — the shades of distinction being fine, you understand. . . . Bears . . . have to be interpreted no less than entrails and birds, and some magical person has to be found to do it. . . . I have no idea what methods he employs — possibly the bear piddles on the floor and he observes portents in the steaming what-not."[4]

Richard Adams's own position seems to be a variant of that of the Grand Inquisitor. "Superstition and accident manifest the will of God," he quotes (from Jung) in his epigraph. Even if the supernatural does not exist, it is good for men to believe in it — not because it makes them behave better, but because it gives shape and purpose to their existence. In *Shardik,* belief causes men to act cruelly and destructively as well as nobly; the bear is a kind of test that brings out hidden strengths and weaknesses, even in those who do not believe in him.

The hero of the novel, the simple hunter Kelderek, who discovers Shardik first, is completely transformed. Following the bear, he becomes first its prophet, then its companion in war, and finally its captor and jailer, the powerful priest-king of Bekla. Power corrupts Kelderek as it does many other characters in the book, though in a different way. Like most ordinary people, Kelderek would not consciously do evil, but he is capable of permitting very unpleasant things to occur outside the range of his immediate attention. In order to support the expensive Beklan war economy and maintain what he thinks of as Shardik's empire (though Shardik is half-mad in a temple dungeon), he allows his merchants to reestablish the slave trade, managing not to hear, or rather not to heed, reports of traders who kidnap and mutilate children.

Later, with the poetic justice that operates less often in contemporary war economies, Kelderek himself becomes a slave in the power of the worst of these traders, a man named Genshed. This section of the book reads so much like a sadistic nightmare that Adams has felt it necessary to disclaim responsibility in a prefatory note: "Lest any should suppose that I set my wits to work to invent the cruelties of Genshed, I say here that all lie within my knowledge and some — would they did not — within my experience."[5] Adams, a former British civil servant, does not say what experience.

Gifted writers of fantasy, even when they disclaim belief in magic, often seem to have a supernatural precognition of historic events, so that their books are more relevant years after they appear than when they were written. H. G. Wells's pretty, silly, commercially exploited Eloi were invented long before the Flower Children appeared; and Aldous Huxley's characters blurred the natural depression caused by his brave new world with Soma well before the discovery of tranquilizers. Authors often disclaim this gift and deny that their books might be read symbolically. Even Tolkien insisted that Frodo's ring of absolute destructive power had nothing to do with modern science or the atomic bomb.

Similarly, Richard Adams would probably claim that no thought of war in Southeast Asia crossed his mind while he was writing *Shardik*. If so, it is merely a lucky coincidence that this brilliant and frightening novel appeared in America at a time when we, like Kelderek, had finally and fully become aware of how much destruction of the natural world and innocent people, how much mutilation and kidnapping of children, had been done in the name of our gods during the preceding twenty years.

15

Games of Dark

WILLIAM MAYNE

For a long time children's books have been the black sheep of serious fiction; like detective stories and westerns, they are tended mainly by specialists, critics of popular culture, or nostalgic sentimentalists. In libraries they are herded together into a separate room, or quarantined from the rest of literature in the stacks under the letters *PZ*.

Occasionally, though, a writer for children appears who is recognized almost at once as having remarkable literary quality. A case in point is William Mayne, one of the most gifted contemporary British writers. His thirty-five years in the field — in this case, you should probably picture a steep, stone-walled pasture in the Yorkshire dales, where Mayne has lived most of his life — have produced picture books, family stories, tales of mystery and adventure, and some of the best fantasy and time-travel fiction to come out of England since Tolkien.

Mayne's dialogue has been likened to Harold Pinter's, his "exploration in depth of sense experience"[1] to that of John Keats, his "alienation devices"[2] to Bertolt Brecht's, and his sensitivity to landscape and primitive emotion to Lawrence's. By and large, these comparisons are not all that far off. Mayne also manages to treat extremely sophisticated ideas and sub-

jects — including the ambiguities of perception and the shifting relations of present and past — in a lucidly simple manner,
so that he can be read by children. If most of juvenile literature, however original and brilliant, were not still largely in
quarantine, he would also be widely read by adults.

Today the style of most children's books is at best clear,
lively, and energetic; at worst it becomes careless, clumsy,
and halting. Mayne's love of language, his accurate, poetic
sense of how words sound and what they mean, therefore
mark him out as, in a sense, subversive. But what he has to
say also goes against convention. His best books suggest that
the history of the British Empire is sometimes not a chronicle
of glory and triumph, but a dark and confused record; that
social, family, and even sexual identity may be fluid; and that
the life of the mind is as real as what we call daily life.

THE FIRST thing about Mayne's work that strikes most critics is the vividness and economy of his language and his acute,
subtle sense of how the world looks and sounds. In *A Game
of Dark*, a story about a boy who loses himself and finds
himself again in an imagined medieval world, fallen leaves are
"circles of faded carpet along the streets, . . . and between
these circles with their unsewn edges lay the starlit desert
of cloudless pavement."[3]

When Mayne describes a train starting, the rhythm of
his sentences is onomatopoetic: "Then there was a sort of
small shake in the engine, and from the wheels there came
a noise like sugar being trodden on, which was the rust on
the rails being powdered. From the engine itself came a puff-
ing roar and there was movement, and then there was
going."[4]

Even the briefest simile can open out: "There was [a
bird] quite near, and he heard its wings flutter against the air
like a book being shaken."[5] The reader, if he or she

chooses — and no doubt some do so choose — can test this comparison by shaking the volume in which it is printed, so that the book becomes the bird. It is the sort of odd reverberation that occurs often in Mayne's work.

He is also astute in describing mental phenomena, as in this meditation by a bedridden boy: "What you see in a dream is like part of you, all the trees are like your own hands and all the ground is like your own feet and the sun is part of your own eyes. There were trees in the garden, but their shadows were just as important; there were birds flying in the air, but the air was just as important."[6]

A related gift of Mayne's is the ability to enter sympathetically into the minds of a wide range of characters. It is perhaps most brilliantly demonstrated in *Salt River Times,* a series of interlocking sketches set in a working-class Australian suburb. With what seems effortless ease, Mayne reproduces the speech and thoughts of an elderly Chinaman, a squabbling married couple, and a whole gallery of children and adolescents, including Kate, who is fascinated by mortality: "Dead? says Kate. Bring them in, the death bed, the death sheet. Does anybody want them. I'll have them. I collect people, feathers, sharks, screams, ghosts. I am the collector. Bring them to me."[7]

Though Mayne's portraits of adults are often skillful, his important characters are usually children or innocents, unsophisticated, half-literate people, separated from the contemporary world in some way — they are gypsies, servants and laborers, farmers in remote Yorkshire villages, or inhabitants of an earlier period of history.

In Mayne's books such protagonists or narrators see nature and human relations uncontaminated by received ideas and speak a language that is both simple and original. They also have the child's or the primitive's relation to time: it is not regulated by clock and calendar, but is free to expand

and contract according to subjective perception. In the mind of the old servingwoman who remembers her girlhood in *Max's Dream*, today and sixty years ago melt into each other.

Several of Mayne's books are marked by an alliance between the very young and the very old, who have clear if idiosyncratic memories of the past and speak to children as equals. Middle-aged people, such as parents and teachers, are often preoccupied and uncomprehending. Their interaction with the child characters is practical: they make rules, set tasks, and pack lunches. When children and parents (or teachers) speak to each other, the tone is detached and cool — sometimes, indeed, Pinteresque. In *A Parcel of Trees*, for instance, Susan (aged fourteen) is sitting on her bed reading one hot day, when her mother challenges her:

> "I don't know how you're going to make out at all," said Mum. "Or I wouldn't if we didn't all feel the same. It's the weather."
>
> "It's the dreadful life we lead," said Susan.
>
> "What do you mean?" said Mum. "You're the dreadful life, lying about like an old stump."
>
> "I haven't any branches," said Susan. "Do you think my soul's died first, and I'm going on automatic?"
>
> "To think you used to be a sweet little girl," said Mum. "I enjoyed having you."[8]

Even between children, real connection is unusual. What matters is not how they feel about each other, but how they feel about themselves and the country or town they live in, or the success of some common enterprise.

Though Mayne often stands back several feet from his characters, his descriptions of Yorkshire are close and loving. He knows its economy of farming and sheep raising, its plants and animals, its weather and seasons. His preference seems to be for late autumn and winter, when the land is bare of leaves and of outsiders:

> It snew the night through and it froze hard. But there were warm spots, like the shippon at milking time with the cows chewing and slopping and the milk cracking in the pail and coming in the dairy with hairy ice round the rim. . . . And there was always this aske wind, that never stopped. Most of the time it blew gentle, but there were days when it hurried on through our gates like the dog was on it, and the snow was stouring and banking up.[9]

As with many other British writers, Mayne's sense of landscape is intertwined with an almost archaeological sense of the past. He rejoices that every field has an ancient name and that popular legends keep old beliefs and events alive. For him history is literally hidden beneath the landscape and may appear at any time, as when Patty in *Underground Alley* discovers a five-hundred-year-old street of houses buried under a hill behind her cellar.

Occasionally the reappearance of the past is supernatural. In *Earthfasts* an eighteenth-century drummer boy called Nellie Jack John emerges into the modern world from beneath a ruined castle, carrying a candle that burns with a cold, unextinguishable light. His interpretation of contemporary events transforms them: "A car started in the market place, went up the steepness in a low gear. . . . 'Wild boars,' said Nellie Jack John. 'They come up by the town of a night.' "[10]

Mayne's fascination with the past is not unique. Much of the population of Britain today appears to be living in the shadow of history, and sometimes — to judge by films, television, and popular literature — heroism, virtue, relevance, even meaning, seem to have ended after World War II. For

Mayne, however, all history is sometimes dark. Patty's "underground alley" turns out to be a decoy built to entrap and destroy a caravan of horses and men carrying treasure from Wales; the bricks of its pavement are gold, but behind the false fronts of its houses lie bones. What is concealed underground, in the past, is often both death and treasure.

William Mayne has now written more than seventy books; as might be expected, his work is uneven. But at his best he is remarkable. Among his most interesting tales are *Winter Quarters,* a moving account of life among contemporary gypsies; and *A Game of Dark,* which can be read either as a time-travel story or the account of a boy on the edge of a mental breakdown.

Winter Quarters, though a realistic narrative, is full of near-magical events. It is the story of the reuniting of a clan of "fairground people" that has been separated and leaderless for fifty years. They have now lost their permission — possibly their right — to camp in a field by the sea for the winter. Lall, a gypsy girl, stays behind with "houseys" when her people are turned away. Instead of attending school, she reads the landscape: "The sheep were walking, standing, in clumps, scattered, lying at random. She herself added a punctuation to the meaningless sentence by standing in a corner of the field . . . on a rustling carpet of frost, while wrens flew about the hedge and bluetits scolded, and she heard the grass tear in sheep teeth."[11] Eventually Lall discovers the buried secrets of her text, which as usual include both death and treasure.

Meanwhile a baby is born with birthmarks that proclaim him to be a chief, and the boy Issy is sent to search for the former chief, who was cast out by the tribe. In the course of his quest Issy meets many strange fairground characters. One, known as Fish, recites a fairground spiel that is also a metaphor of Issy's search:

"These are the original Sumatran Invisible Fish, and I had three this morning, but as you can tell there are now four, another one has hatched, what a sight, absolutely transparent except when they close their eyes, very rare. You get a better view if you close yours, that's it. . . . You understand, you are invisible to them when you have your eyes open. So blink gently."[12]

The undernote of the book is semiotic: the need to name the world before it can be known. As Issy puts it, "A thing is hard to see until you know what you are looking at. You have to be able to imagine it at the same time."[13] In a hall of mirrors he has another kind of vision — a new reading, if you like, of his other self.

It was a tall, distorted, mangled reflection of himself, uncannily tall, a spindly stranger. When he put out his arm to its full length the pathetic monster in the glass put out a slow stub and could do no more.

And does this part of me, he wondered, try to come out from beyond the glass, being thrown back injured time after time? Am I like that, now and then?[14]

Clearly, he is; and the old chief, too, turns out to have a strange, variously named, shifting identity.

The hero of *A Game of Dark* also has two selves. He is a fourteen-year-old English schoolboy called Donald Jackson, deeply alienated from his narrowly religious parents. Though the book was published in 1971, it is prescient in its portrait of an adolescent out of touch with reality and absorbed in a Dungeons and Dragons type of imaginary world. It can also be read as a tale in the tradition of Jorge Luis Borges or Gabriel García Márquez, in which fantastic events are simultaneously real and metaphoric.

Donald's mother is an exhausted, priggish, and disapproving schoolteacher whom he cannot seem to please. His father is a half-paralyzed invalid, white-faced and white-haired, angry, hypercritical, and rigid in his faith. He and his wife read his affliction as a judgment or test: " 'There was never much wrong physically,' said Mrs. Jackson. 'We knew it was a visitation from God. . . . It was put upon us for our own good.' "15 Donald knows he should love and pity his father, but cannot: "What he noticed most about the pain Mr. Jackson had to bear was his own inability to appreciate and understand it. It meant to him a white-faced man of uncertain temper and dour disposition."16

Later he begins to fantasize that he is not the son of Mr. and Mrs. Jackson: "If he had been taken in by them, adopted . . . , that might account for the way he turned out not to please them. . . . If the man called Daddy was not his father, and the woman called Mum not his mother, then he had no need to feel guilty for no longer loving them as parents."17

When Donald goes to visit his father in the hospital, he feels he is in a "bedroom that he had no right to be in."18 Mr. Jackson, blurred by drugs, also denies his son's existence, though he remembers Donald's sister, who died before Donald was born; and Mrs. Jackson reinforces the denial:

> "Hello, boy," said Mr. Jackson, in a slow drawling tone. "Where's Cecily?"
> "She's all right," said Mrs. Jackson. "She couldn't come today."19

Finally, approaching the hospital on his next visit, Donald imagines his father lying inside and rejects him wholly: "That patch of life was not even a person at present, not even intelligence, and most of all it had nothing to do with his own existence, he had nothing to do with it; he had no feelings about it except revulsion."20

But though they increase during the book, Donald's misery and disorientation are evident from the first line: "Donald heard Mr. Savery shouting at him: 'Jackson, what's the matter?' Donald tried to speak, but he had no throat to speak with and nothing to say, nothing that he knew about."[21] "The days are just happening," he says at one point. "I can't do anything about them."[22] His surroundings seem unreal, and he seems unreal to himself: "Donald sat in the vacuum of indoors and heard the weather being pumped past, as if it were emptying the building and increasing the internal vacuum."[23]

While he goes passively through the motions of living, Donald moves in and out of another world in which he is known as Jackson and is active, competent, and loved. Here he comes upon a medieval town threatened by a huge dragon or worm: icy cold, death-white, with an unbearable stench and a slimy track twenty feet wide. At first Donald realizes that this world is fantasy: "One is real, he said to himself. Donald is real. The other is a game of darkness, and I can be either and step from one to the other as I like."[24] Soon his two worlds become equally real. In the medieval town he becomes the trusted squire of the local lord, and then a knight. Naturally, he begins to prefer this world: "He was seeing both places, and could again choose which to take. He chose the one with less shame and guilt to it."[25]

It is clear that Donald's alternate world, real or not, is a metaphor for the real one. The worm stands for violence and hatred; but it is also a version of his father, a death-white, cold, crawling phallic horror (Mr. Jackson, like the monster, cannot walk) whose entire will is toward destruction. The girl Carrica, whom Donald rescues from the worm and who comes to love him, is both his mother at an earlier age and his lost sister, Cecily.

The lord Donald serves is an idealized version of Berry,

the good-natured Anglican vicar. Both of them stand for order and reason: "an accepted way of doing things, a framework in which to live and achieve the best."[26] It is a limited vision, which underestimates the power of evil. Gradually, Donald comes to see Berry's tolerance as senseless: "The meeting [of the church Youth Guild] had been what Berry called an open-ended argument, so open-ended that anything put into it fell right through without affecting what was being talked about."[27] The lord is equally limited. "With a proper administrative setup," he remarks at one point, "the worm would probably leave of its own accord."[28]

The worm does not leave, but at first its taking of human life is controlled by providing livestock for it to devour. Eventually, however, the villagers begin to run out of cows and sheep, and the lord must fight the worm. He approaches it bravely, in the traditional way, and fails: "The orderliness had at last killed him, because the accepted way of dealing with worms had been fatal," Jackson thinks.[29]

It is left to Jackson to destroy the worm, which he does by craft at the very end of the book. Meanwhile, in his other life, his father has come home from the hospital and is lying ill in the room next door, breathing loudly and raspingly, so that Donald cannot sleep, haunting the place as the worm does the medieval town. "The whole life of the house, the whole intent of the day, seemed to centre on him, or on something near him, his illness."[30]

Jackson's triumph is flawed; the worm "was slain in unfair combat, and no glory from its death could come to him."[31] "It was not an honorable deed," he says to Carrica.[32] Yet afterward Donald can see his two worlds clearly for the first time: "Half of him watched the house in Hales Hill. Half looked at the girl, Carrica. . . . She was his mother or his sister, . . . and he knew that the man in the other room was his father, whom he knew now how to love. Carrica was a phantom if he wanted her to be, and the house in Hales Hill was another, and he had the choice of which to remain with."[33]

Just after he has chosen to return to the present-day world, his father dies in the next room: "There was no breathing. Donald lay and listened to the quiet, and went to sleep, consolate."[34] This is the end of the book, an ending that has puzzled and disturbed critics. The supernatural explanation would be that Donald killed his father when he slew the worm; he will know "how to love" Mr. Jackson now because Mr. Jackson will be dead. A more naturalistic reading might suggest that once Donald realizes his father is dying, he no longer needs to hate and fear him.

On another level, we as readers repeat Donald's experience. While we are engaged with the book, we are passive in the "real" world and active in imagination: the bird flies as the pages are shaken. When we reach the end of the story and return to reality, the characters become phantoms; in a sense, we have killed them.

One of the strengths of the story is that it holds all these readings, and no doubt others, in suspension. *A Game of Dark*, like all of William Mayne's best work, and most serious fiction, adult or "juvenile," does not end neatly. Instead it opens out possibility and meaning.

16

The Folklore of Childhood

One of the most striking things about children's books is how widely they are known by adults. Probably almost everyone in America and Britain today is familiar with "Cinderella" and *Alice's Adventures in Wonderland;* not one in ten will have read James Joyce.

The universality and antiquity of children's folklore — rhymes, games, jokes, and superstitions — are even more amazing. Half the rhymes in *Mother Goose,* for instance, were current before 1700, and 90 percent of them before 1800. Children today play games that are known in tribal Africa and were familiar in ancient Rome. When a child climbs a pile of stones and shouts "I'm the king of the castle, get down you dirty rascal!" he is repeating a Roman children's taunt; when an older girl or boy shows a baby the "two little birds, sitting on a hill, one named Jack and the other named Jill," she or he is rehearsing a nursery entertainment known on four continents.

As studies like Iona and Peter Opie's classic *The Singing Game* show, children's games and rhymes and jokes do not exist in isolation: they have echoes in history, anthropology, archaeology, literature, popular culture, and art. The Opies, among others, have pointed out connections between games found on contemporary playgrounds and ancient pagan customs. "London Bridge," for example, traditionally ends with a watchman being set to guard the bridge, after which it remains standing. They relate this to an ancient and sister tradition:

> It has long been thought sensible to propitiate the river with a sacrifice, a human life if possible. . . . A foundation sacrifice of human bones and the bones of cattle and sheep was found beneath an arch of Old Blackfriars Bridge, built 1760–8; and as recently as 1939 an engineer constructing a bridge in Assam was brought a live month-old baby to build into the foundations. ("My Indian workmen were most enthusiastic.")[1]

For the last hundred years or more, according to the Opies, singing games have been played mainly by seven- to ten-year-old girls, with older and younger children, and an occasional boy, joining in now and then. They are thus a contemporary instance of the traditional transmission of oral culture by females, which makes it no surprise that some of their verses express scorn for men and their expectations:

> Silly old man, he walks alone,
> He wants a wife and he can't get one.[2]

> What's for dinner, luv,
> What's for dinner, luv, farewell?
> . . . .
> Bread and butter and beetles,
> And you shall have some.[3]

Several games act out a drama in which suitors come seeking a bride and are repeatedly refused. It's only fair to add, however, that they usually succeed in the end, and that they occasionally refuse the brides offered them — once, notably, in a verse that suggests disillusion with the current health-club, beach-animal type:

> They are all too black and brawny,
> They sit in the sun uncloudy,
> With golden chains around their necks,
> They are too black and brawny.[4]

The potential for violence in women is also acknowledged:

> Round apples, round apples,
> By night and by day.
> There stands a valley
> In yonder haze.
> There stands [Moira Rogers]
> With a knife in her hand,
> You dare not touch her
> Or else she'll be hanged.[5]

Many writers over the years have recognized the power of these old songs and games and used them to considerable effect. A striking example of this that the Opies do not mention occurs in L. P. Hartley's most famous ghost story, "A Visitor from Down Under." Its hero, Victor Rumbold, has just arrived in London from Australia, where he has made a fortune by dubious means. He is pursued by the ghost or corpse of a man who is from "down under" in a more sinister sense: James Hagberd, whom he has murdered. Hagberd makes his presence known through a singing game heard over the radio on a children's program:

> The chant throbbed into a war-cry.

> Who will you have for your Nuts and May,
>   Nuts and May, Nuts and May;
> Who will you have for your Nuts and May
>   On a cold and frosty morning?

They would have Victor Rumbold for Nuts and
May, Victor Rumbold, Victor Rumbold: and from the
vindictiveness in their voices they might have meant to
have had his blood, too.

And who will you send to fetch him away,
    Fetch him away, fetch him away;
Who will you send to fetch him away
    On a cold and frosty morning?

Like a clarion call, a shout of defiance, came the
reply:

We'll send Jimmy Hagberd to fetch him away,
    Fetch him away, fetch him away;
We'll send Jimmy Hagberd to fetch him away
    On a wet and foggy evening.[6]

What makes this especially effective is the shudder we feel
at the juxtaposition of childhood play with wickedness and
revenge from beyond the grave.*

The illusion of adults that children not only should but
can be shielded somehow from knowledge of unpleasant realities might be rapidly dissolved if they were to listen to some
of the verses the Opies and other scholars like Francelia
Butler and Simon J. Bronner have collected. Everything we
might want to protect boys and girls from is already in these
verses, where it is treated with an almost comic detachment.
Violent death (from Southend-on-Sea, England):

Look, look, mama,
What is that stuff
That looks like strawberry jam?

---

*The connection of "Nuts and May," according to the Opies, with
medieval May games and mock marriage by capture gives the verses an
additional uneasy resonance.

Hush, hush, my child,
It is papa,
Run over by a tram.[7]

Alcoholism (from Belfast):

My Aunt Fannie
She walks very canny,
For she isn't very steady
On her feet.
She spends all her money
Drinking with her honey
At the pub at the corner
Of the street.[8]

Pregnancy and birth (United States):

My mommy lies over the ocean
My daddy lies over the sea
My daddy lies over my mommy
And that's how they got little me.[9]

The welfare state (United States):

I made you look
You dirty crook
You stole your momma's food stamp book.
Turn it in, turn it out
Now you know what welfare's all about.[10]

And, finally, modern warfare (United States):

Little Bo-Peep
Has lost her sheep
And thinks they may be roaming.
They haven't fled,
They've all dropped dead
From nerve gas in Wyoming.[11]

Though these verses carry a clear message, to an adult much of the folklore of childhood may sound trivial or even meaningless. This is to make the same kind of mistake that early explorers made when they couldn't understand the stories and jokes told in other cultures. Later on, anthropologists who took the time to study these societies understood their folklore — indeed, studying the folklore was one of the ways they came to understand the society.

Anyone who has spent time around children and observed them carefully, or really remembers what it was like to be a child, knows that childhood is also a separate culture, with its own rituals, beliefs, games, and customs, and its own, largely oral, literature. Childhood, in this sense, is a primitive society — or rather, several primitive societies, one leading into the other. Ontogeny recapitulates phylogeny; the development of the individual parallels the development of the race.

Just as the stages of the human embryo repeat the stages of human evolution, so that at one point the embryo has gills and later a tail, the social development of the individual child repeats that of the human species. The earliest stage is that of prehistoric man and woman, or prehistoric baby. This creature is a savage whose principal interest is survival. Socially his or her world is very small, usually limited to the immediate family, and he/she is preverbal — he/she cannot speak but communicates in sign language or with inarticulate cries.

Next come ancient man and woman, socialized to the extent that they can function in small groups, as a two- or three-year-old does. Anthropologists studying primitive societies believe that this is often a matriarchal stage, in which the important authority figures are women. In the same way, the important people in a toddler's world are apt to be mother, baby-sitter, grandmother, and perhaps a nursery-school teacher. Occasionally a teacher or a sitter may be male, and father or grandfather may be around in a way that counts; but even today such cases are unusual.

The primitive toddler also has a strong and close relationship and identification with certain animals, which can be compared to totemism. The child considers the family dog or cat as a rational being, talks to it, imitates its behavior. The toddler also, like ancient man and woman, lives in what might be called a hunting-and-gathering economy, in which daily exploration of his/her territory — and at times, defense of this territory from others — plays an important part. And like primitive man and woman, the toddler is pre-literate.

The final stage of childhood, from about six to twelve, corresponds to early civilization. Here the central social group is not the family, but the gang or tribe. It is in this stage that we see the development of myth and ritual — passwords, charms and spells, counting-out rhymes, formulaic games. Its literature, like the literature of other developing societies, is largely an unwritten one. These cultures often develop some form of writing, and a fair proportion of the population may be able to read and write a little, but they don't do it for fun.

It is a society that believes, or half believes, in magic and is rich in superstitions, such as the one about the Awful Stuff in the center of every golf ball, a sort of explosive acid that if you cut down into the ball will get out and destroy everything around. Also widespread is the warning not to swing high enough on the school playground to go over the bar: if you do, you will turn inside out. Children may not quite believe these warnings, but they still pass them on to younger children.

Some of the superstitions of childhood have a kind of symbolic truth to them. For instance, when a child makes an awful face, another child is apt to tell her that she'd better not do that or it will stick on her for life. In terms of the immediate situation, of course, this is a lie. But it is quite true that if your customary expression is unpleasant, eventually the lines of frowning or sneering or bullying will etch themselves into your face, just as the habit of disapproving or sneering or bullying will etch itself into your character.

Children still have an active folk culture, which like that of preliterate or semiliterate societies everywhere is handed on from one generation to another. Their verses, their beliefs, their games, are vitally important to them — otherwise they would not survive. Like all folklore, these parts of the culture express the basic emotions and fill the basic needs of a community.

One function of folklore is to help its users to understand and if possible to control the world — or at least to feel that they are controlling it — and one way to control the world, of course, is with words. To a small child, words are magical. To quote Martha Wolfenstein, whose book *Children's Humor*, though written more than twenty-five years ago, is still a classic, "The child feels that in learning the names of persons and things he gains a marvelous power over them. When he calls the name of a person, does not that person come to him? When he calls the name of a thing, is it not supplied?"[12]

Imagine a baby on the verge of learning to speak. For all of her life she has been inarticulate — she wants something, but all she can do is cry or say "Uh, uh, uh!" Then, somehow, the purpose of speech is revealed to her, and after what must be a tremendous struggle, the power of speech. Though we all once experienced it, it is hard now to picture the immense thrill of power we must have felt the first time we cried "Mommy!" or "Cookie!" and saw what we desired appear. From this experience, surely, comes the power of magic words and spells in fairy tales.

Small children like simple, repetitive rhymes and games, just as they like repetitive or cumulative folktales such as "The Gingerbread Man." As they grow older and more competent linguistically they become impatient with such tales; they learn that the magic spell doesn't always work and that words don't always mean what they seem to mean.

At this point, between the ages of six and ten, we begin to get riddles and puns and jokes based on the tricks and confusions of language. The attraction of the riddle is that the person who asks it demonstrates her or his mastery of the ambiguity that is built into language. For instance:

— What has four legs and can't walk?
— A table.

A riddle can also be a device for proving the other person stupid — in some cases, stupid because he or she takes riddles seriously.

— What's the difference between a mailbox and a hole in the ground?
— I don't know.
— Well, I certainly wouldn't send you to mail a letter.

Eventually children learn that words can be used to excuse misbehavior, and even as a way of trapping a victim into a kind of complicity with his or her persecutor — which is something a lot of adults do with children, getting them to agree that they've been bad and deserve to be punished, for instance. This use of language seems to be behind a familiar catch-riddle:

— Adam and Eve and Pinchme went out in a boat to swim. Adam and Eve got drowned, and who was left?

The correct answer maneuvers the victim into asking to be hurt. But there is more to this joke. Its three characters, Adam and Eve and Pinchme, suggest primal, innocent man and woman — or boy and girl — and someone who represents evil, violent impulse, knowledge of good and evil: the serpent in the garden.

As children get older they discover other tricks of language. They become fascinated with tongue twisters, with secret languages like Pig Latin, and with simile and metaphor. Some years ago, for instance, there was a whole cycle of jokes about a character called the Little Moron; the point of the joke was always that he misunderstood metaphors and took them for reality:

— Why did the Little Moron throw the clock out the window?
— Because he wanted to see time fly.

In telling this joke the child asserts that he is not a little moron; he knows what a metaphor is and no longer takes it literally. But the joke also, like a lot of folklore, allows the vicarious expression of forbidden impulses: in this case, the rage children feel when some adult points to the clock as a reason for going to bed, or not having lunch. "No, dear; see, the clock says it's not time yet." No wonder the child wants to throw the clock out the window, to make time fly.

Often the mastery of metaphor is used against adults — even against unknown adults. This happens with the telephone jokes that are played by girls and boys when they begin to acquire a more adult voice — or at least the ability to imitate one. They can then spend happy hours calling up

numbers at random and saying, for example: "Good after-
noon, ma'am. This is the electric company. Would you please
check to see if your refrigerator is running?" The hope is that
the person on the other end of the line will hurry into their
kitchen to check, hurry back, pick up the phone again, and
confirm that it is. Then the reply is: "Well, you'd better catch
it before it runs out the door." If the joke works, the caller
has the satisfaction of making the adult follow a child's directions and look silly.

Jokes and riddles are not the only types of folklore that
allow the release of forbidden wishes and feelings. Rhymes,
for instance, often express sibling rivalry, especially between
the sexes. Here is a jump-rope rhyme known in both Britain
and America:

> Johnny over the ocean,
> Johnny over the sea,
> [Johnny] broke a teacup
> And blamed it on me.
> I told Ma,
> Ma told Pa,
> Johnny got a licking,
> Ha, ha, ha.

This is fairly sophisticated: the antisocial act is performed by
someone else, who then wickedly tries to shift the guilt but
fails. The little girl complains to her mother, the mother
reports to the father, the father deals out the punishment,
and Johnny's sister triumphs, at least in imagination.

Resentment of teachers is an especially popular theme,
and more apt to be overt. There are dozens of rhymes like
the following one, which takes off from and mocks the many
verses that kind educators have invented to help children
learn arithmetic:

Twelve and twelve are twenty-four,
Kick the teacher out the door.
If she tries to come back in,
Throw her in the garbage bin,
If she tells you "Don't do that,"
Hit her with a baseball bat.

Other rhymes are more subtle:

The Devil flew from north to south
With [Miss Johnson] in his mouth.
And when he found she was a fool
He dropped her onto [Fall Creek] School.

Most teachers do not find this amusing, but children think it is uproarious.

As Martha Wolfenstein says, the joke that seems funny to a child may not seem funny to adults, or to children of different ages. The general rule seems to be that as you grow older the forbidden wish or emotion is gradually more disguised, and the joke that allows it expression becomes more complicated.

For example, take the natural interest that children have in their own and other people's bodies. Preschoolers will often spontaneously pull their skirts up or their jeans down to show you their tummies, or lie on their backs waving their legs about and giggling. By the time they start school, this sort of activity has mostly been given up. Instead, children of six or so tease others by trying to pull down their pants; they now know they are not supposed to expose themselves, so they try to expose someone else.

At about seven, actual physical assault is replaced by rhymes about exposure. There are literally dozens of these, most along the lines of:

I see England, I see France,
I see [Mary's] underpants.

To the adult such verses seem stupid and, if one has to hear them very often, annoying. But to the child, as Wolfenstein points out, they represent a giant step toward growing up. The conflict between id and superego, between the wish to see and show off nakedness and the knowledge that this is naughty and forbidden, has been sublimated into art. It is a very low form of art, but art nevertheless.

A year or two later, at about age eight, we begin to get verses about the nakedness of absent or fictional persons — another level of sophistication. Children this age recite rhymes like:

Hi-ho Silver everywhere,
Tonto lost his underwear.

At nine or ten children get to the point where simply announcing the physical exposure of someone doesn't feel right; there has to be an excuse for the event. So we get a new sort of rhyme. Here, for instance, is a taunt that uses the name of the victim's mother:

[Mrs. Smith] went to town,
To buy a pair of britches,
When she came home she tried them on
And bang went all the stitches.

Another charm of this one, no doubt, is that the person exposed is a parent, an authority figure.

By eleven or twelve most children have given up reciting such verses, but they still enjoy jokes and stories about physical exposure, especially if it happens as a result of an accident. Sometimes they will tell a story in which one of the characters is a younger child who doesn't know something about the world that they have recently learned. Such a tale has a double payoff: it works, a psychologist might say, both in Freudian and in Adlerian terms (sexual release — superiority). For example:

> Once there was a little girl walking home from school, and she met a man on the street, and he said to her, "Little girl, can you stand on your head?" So she said yes, and he said, "If you'll stand on your head now, I'll give you ten cents." So she did, and he did. But when she got home she told her mother, and her mother was indignant. "You shouldn't have done that," her mother said. "All he wanted was to see your underpants." Well, the next day when the little girl got home from school, her mother asked if she met the nasty man who wanted to see her underpants. So the little girl said, "Yes, and he gave me ten cents today, too. But I fooled him. I didn't wear any."

FOLKLORE IS not only a medium helping its audience to understand and control a world and allowing the release of forbidden impulses; it is also the oldest form of the arts. Before there were paintings and symphonies and ballets there were beautiful woven cloths and baskets, haunting tunes, and ceremonial dances. Before there were novels and television shows there were legends and ballads, which everybody in the society knew and repeated. Today, unfortunately, most of us are consumers rather than producers of the arts; and a lot of what we consume, though it goes down easily, is secondhand and second-rate. Or else it is so complicated and intellectual that it doesn't have much impact: we have to work to understand it and maybe work even harder to like it.

Children, however, are still living partly in a folk culture.

They are still actively inventing and passing on stories and verses, some of which have the simplicity, originality, and profundity of great folk literature. For instance, here is a rhyme that was collected more than fifty years ago and is still current:

> My mother told me I never should
> Play with the gypsies in the wood,
> The wood was dark, the grass was green,
> In came Sally with a tambourine.
> I came to a river and I couldn't get across,
> I paid ten dollars for an old white horse,
> I jumped on his back and gave him a crack —
> Sally, tell my mother I shall never come back.

Notice how elegantly economical and indirect this is. It is the same story as the ballad of Gypsy Davy or the Wraggle-Taggle Gypsies, but extremely condensed.

Here's another rhyme that is very old and still current. Its subject is also metaphor, but metaphor continually turning into reality:

> A man of words and not of deeds
>   is like a garden full of weeds,
> And when the weeds begin to grow
>   it's like a garden full of snow,
> And when the snow begins to melt
>   it's like a garden full of felt,
> And when the felt begins to peel
>   it's like a garden full of steel,
> And when the steel begins to rust
>   it's like a garden full of dust,
> And when the dust begins to fly
>   it's like an eagle in the sky,
> And when the sky begins to roar

it's like a lion at your door,
And when your door begins to crack
it's like a stick across your back,
And when your back begins to smart
it's like a whip across your heart,
And when your heart begins to fail
it's like a ship without a sail,
And when the sail begins to sink
it's like a bottle full of ink,
And when the ink begins to write
it makes the paper all black and white.

It is interesting that what finally stops the magic chain is writing it down, moving from oral to written poetry.

Too often, as we leave the tribal culture of childhood — and its sometimes subversive tales and rhymes — behind, we lose contact with instinctive joy in self-expression: with the creative imagination, spontaneous emotion, and the ability to see the world as full of wonders. Staying in touch with children's literature and folklore as an adult is not only a means of understanding what children are thinking and feeling; it is a way of understanding and renewing our own childhood.

Notes

1 / SUBVERSIVE CHILDREN'S LITERATURE (pp. 3–15)

1. Mark Twain, *The Adventures of Tom Sawyer*, p. 54.
2. Ibid., p. ix.
3. Lewis Carroll, *Through the Looking-Glass, and What Alice Found There*, p. 126.
4. Ibid., p. 124.
5. Ibid., p. 189.
6. Carroll, *Alice's Adventures in Wonderland*, p. 187.
7. Carroll, *Through the Looking-Glass*, p. 212.
8. Quoted in James Blair, *Mark Twain and Huck Finn*, p. 339.
9. Kenneth Grahame, *The Wind in the Willows*, p. 251. For a very interesting analysis of Grahame's contrasting visions of the ideal life as portrayed in Rat and Toad, see Roger Sale's *Fairy Tales and After*.
10. Munro Leaf, *The Story of Ferdinand*, unpaged.
11. P. L. Travers, *Mary Poppins Comes Back*, p. 3.
12. Ibid., p. 7.
13. Rudyard Kipling, *Recessional* (1899), stanza 4.
14. L. F. Baum, *The Wonderful Wizard of Oz*, pp. 12–13.
15. Ibid., p. 189.
16. Henry M. Littlefield, "The Wizard of Oz: Parable on Populism," *American Quarterly*, Spring 1964.
17. Louisa May Alcott, *Little Women*, p. 10.
18. Dr. Seuss, *The Cat in the Hat*, pp. 60–61.

2 / FOLKTALE LIBERATION (pp. 16-28)

1. Sarah Trimmer, quoted in Margaret Maxwell, "The Perils of the Imagination: Pre-Victorian Children's Literature and the Critics," *Children's Literature in Education,* vol. 13 (1974): 45–52.
2. Lucy Sprague Mitchell, *The Here and Now Story Book,* p. 21.
3. Ibid., p. 137.
4. See the foreword to the second edition of 1819.
5. See Ruth B. Bottigheimer's fascinating study, *Grimms' Bad Girls and Bold Boys: The Moral and Social Vision of the Tales.* Also John M. Ellis, *One Fairy Story Too Many,* and *The Brothers Grimm and Folktale,* edited by James M. McGlathery, especially the essays by Donald Ward and Ruth B. Bottigheimer.
6. See the excellent and perceptive study by Jack Zipes, *The Trials and Tribulations of Little Red Riding Hood.*
7. Bruno Bettelheim, *The Uses of Enchantment,* p. 32.
8. Jacob and Wilhelm Grimm, *The Juniper Tree and Other Tales from Grimm,* p. 12.
9. Ibid., p. 230.
10. J.R.R. Tolkien, *Tree and Leaf,* p. 43.

3 / FAIRY TALE FICTION: FITZGERALD TO UPDIKE (pp. 29-40)

1. F. Scott Fitzgerald, *Tender Is the Night,* p. 52.
2. Philip Roth, *Portnoy's Complaint,* pp. 4–5.
3. Ibid., p. 11.
4. John Updike, *Of the Farm,* p. 97.
5. Ibid., p. 86.
6. Ibid., p. 31.
7. Ibid., p. 161.
8. Ibid., p. 154.
9. Ibid., p. 40.
10. Ibid., p. 23.
11. Ibid., pp. 140–141.

12. Ibid., p. 134.
13. Ibid., p. 135.

4 / BRAKING FOR ELVES: FASHIONABLE FOLKLORE FOR ADULTS (pp. 41–50)

1. John Updike, *The Coup,* pp. 139–141.
2. Nancy Arrowsmith and George Moorse, *A Field Guide to the Little People,* p. 119.
3. Wil Huygen, *Gnomes,* unpaged.
4. Ibid.
5. A third volume, *Giants,* directed apparently more toward children, in spite of several terrifying illustrations, appeared in 1979.

5 / THE CHILD WHO FOLLOWED THE PIPER: KATE GREENAWAY (pp. 51–66)

1. Quoted in Engen, *Kate Greenaway: A Biography,* p. 141.
2. Ibid., p. 19.
3. Ibid.
4. Ibid., p. 8.
5. Ibid., p. 46.
6. Ibid., p. 26.
7. I am indebted to my friend James Merrill for this observation.
8. Engen, *Kate Greenaway,* p. 67.
9. Ibid., p. 67.
10. Ibid., p. 69.
11. Ibid., p. 64.
12. Ibid., p. 70.
13. Ibid., p. 90.
14. Ibid., p. 103.
15. Ibid., pp. 93–94.
16. Ibid., p. 90.
17. Ibid., p. 76.
18. Ibid., p. 64.
19. Ibid., p. 105.
20. Ibid., p. 108.

21. Ibid., p. 77.
22. Ibid., p. 87.
23. Ibid., p. 132.
24. Ibid., p. 109.
25. Ibid., p. 136.
26. M. H. Spielmann and G. S. Layard, *Kate Greenaway*, p. 258.
27. Engen, *Kate Greenaway*, p. 109.
28. Kate Greenaway, *A Apple Pie*.
29. See Opie, *The Oxford Dictionary of Nursery Rhymes*, p. 47.
30. Engen, *Kate Greenaway*, p. 141.
31. Robert Browning, *The Pied Piper of Hamelin*, p. 14.
32. Ibid., pp. 43–45.
33. Ibid., p. 47.
34. Engen, *Kate Greenaway*, p. 145.
35. Ibid., p. 148.
36. Ibid., p. 145.
37. Ibid., p. 151.
38. Spielmann and Layard, *Kate Greenaway*, p. 260.

6 / TALES OF TERROR: MRS. CLIFFORD (pp. 67–73)

1. "Wooden Tony" was originally published in a book of adult tales, *The Last Touches* (1892). It was included in the second edition of *Anyhow Stories, Moral and Otherwise* (1899).
2. Lucy Lane Clifford, *Aunt Anne*, pp. 24–25.
3. Clifford, *Anyhow Stories*, p. 87.
4. Ibid., pp. 74–75.
5. Clifford, *The Last Touches*, p. 223.
6. Ibid., p. 227.
7. Ibid., p. 229.
8. Ibid., p. 230.
9. Ibid., pp. 240–241.
10. Clifford, *Anyhow Stories*, p. 12.
11. Ibid., p. 24.
12. Ibid., p. 22.
13. Ibid., p. 26.
14. Ibid., p. 38.

15. Ibid., p. 39.
16. Ibid., p. 44.
17. Ibid., p. 47.

7 / FORD MADOX FORD'S FAIRY TALES (pp. 74–89)

1. Arthur Mizener, *The Saddest Story, A Biography of Ford Madox Ford*, p. 68.
2. Ford H. Madox Hueffer, *The Brown Owl, A Fairy Story*, with two illustrations by F. Madox Brown. Published as vol. 1 of The Children's Library. Ford's original name was Hueffer; he changed it legally in 1919, partly to avoid the then-current prejudice against Germanic surnames. Although *The Brown Owl* actually appeared in 1891, it was postdated, as was common at that time, especially for children's books.
3. Mizener, *The Saddest Story*, p. 17.
4. See David Dow Harvey, *Ford Madox Ford, 1873–1939, Bibliography of Works and Criticism*, p. 275.
5. "The Morphology of the French Fairy Tale: The Ethical Model," in *Patterns in Oral Literature*, eds. Heda Jason and Dimitri Segal, p. 50.
6. Hueffer, *The Brown Owl*, p. 18.
7. Ibid., p. 50.
8. Gog and Magog are traditional giants whose statues stand in the Guildhall, London.
9. Hueffer, *The Brown Owl*, p. 66.
10. Ford Madox Ford, *Memories and Impressions*, p. 246.
11. Ibid.
12. Juliet M. Soskice, *Chapters from Childhood*, p. 30.
13. Ford H. Madox Hueffer, *The Feather*, with frontispiece by F. Madox Brown. Published as vol. 10 of The Children's Library. According to Ford's bibliographer, it appeared on October 8, 1892, to a less than enthusiastic critical reception.
14. Ibid., p. 141.
15. Ibid., pp. 84–85.
16. Ibid., p. 181.
17. Ibid., p. 182.
18. Mizener, *The Saddest Story*, p. 24.

19. Ford Huffer [*sic*], *The Queen Who Flew, A Fairy Tale,* with a frontispiece by Sir E. Burne-Jones. It was probably published on May 8, 1894.

20. Mizener, *The Saddest Story,* p. 33. Ford's first book of poems, *The Questions at the Well,* had appeared in 1893.

21. Huffer, *The Queen Who Flew,* p. 59.

22. Harvey, *Ford Madox Ford,* p. 277.

23. Georges Schreiber, *Portraits and Self-Portraits,* pp. 39–40; quoted in Mizener, *The Saddest Story,* p. xiv.

24. Huffer, *The Queen Who Flew,* p. 59.

25. Timothy Weiss, *Fairy Tale and Romance in the Works of Ford Madox Ford,* pp. 32–33.

26. Hueffer, *Christina's Fairy Book;* it appeared in December of that year. I have not seen a copy of this edition. The references that follow are to a later edition: Ford Madox Ford, *Christina's Fairy Book,* illustrated by Jennetta Vise (London: Latimer House, 1949).

27. Ibid., pp. 7–8 (the poem originally appeared in the *Athenaeum,* on October 26, 1901).

28. Ibid., p. 9.

29. Ibid., p. 13.

30. Ibid., p. 30.

31. Ibid., p. 52.

32. Ibid., p. 46.

33. Both these books, *The Benefactor* and *The Soul of London,* were later published.

34. Hueffer, *Christina's Fairy Book,* p. 54.

35. Ibid., p. 60.

36. Mizener, *The Saddest Story,* p. 97.

37. Ezra Pound, "Ford Madox Ford," *New Directions,* no. 7 (1942), p. 480, quoted in Mizener, *The Saddest Story,* p. xiv.

38. Hueffer, *Christina's Fairy Book,* p. 60.

8 / ANIMAL LIBERATION: BEATRIX POTTER (pp. 90–98)

1. Quoted in Margaret Lane, *The Tale of Beatrix Potter,* p. 32.

2. Ibid., p. 28.

3. Beatrix Potter, *The Journal of Beatrix Potter*, 25 April 1883, p. 38.
4. Ibid., 4 October 1884, p. 104.
5. Potter, *The Tale of Peter Rabbit*, p. 59.
6. Suzanne Rahn, "Tailpiece: The Tale of Two Bad Mice," *Children's Literature*, vol. 12, pp. 78–91.
7. Potter, *The Tale of Pigling Bland*, p. 63.
8. Ibid., pp. 77–78.
9. Edward Lear, *Nonsense Songs, Stories, Botany, and Alphabets*, unpaged.

9 / MODERN MAGIC: E. NESBIT (pp. 99–117)

1. Moore, *E. Nesbit*, p. 25.
2. Ibid., p. 182.
3. Ibid., p. 177.
4. Ibid., pp. 208–209.
5. George MacDonald, *The Princess and Curdie*, p. 41.
6. E. Nesbit, *The Story of the Treasure Seekers*, p. 136.
7. Nesbit, "Kenneth and the Carp," *The Magic World*, p. 246.
8. Nesbit, *Five of Us, and Madeline*, p. 38.
9. Nesbit, *Nine Unlikely Tales*, p. 7.
10. Nesbit, *Five of Us, and Madeline*, p. 172.
11. Ibid.
12. Nesbit, *The Magic World*, p. 46.
13. Nesbit, *The Book of Dragons*, pp. 58–60.
14. Nesbit, *Five Children and It*, p. 20.
15. Nesbit, *The Magic World*, pp. 112–113.
16. Nesbit, *Nine Unlikely Tales*, p. 205.
17. Nesbit, *The Story of the Amulet*, p. 212.
18. Ibid., pp. 195–196.
19. Nesbit, *The Book of Dragons*, p. 37.
20. Ibid., p. 4.
21. Nesbit, *Five of Us, and Madeline*, p. 49.
22. Nesbit, *Five Children and It*, p. 19.
23. Nesbit, *The Enchanted Castle*, p. 85.
24. Nesbit, *Nine Unlikely Tales*, p. 19.
25. Ibid., p. 46.
26. Nesbit, *The Enchanted Castle*, p. 187.

27. Ibid., p. 226.
28. Ibid., pp. 228–229.
29. Ibid., p. 237.
30. Ibid., p. 240.
31. Ibid., p. 240.
32. Ibid., p. 243.
33. Ibid., p. 31.

10 / THE BOY WHO COULDN'T GROW UP: JAMES BARRIE (pp. 118–135)

1. James Barrie, *The Works of J. M. Barrie*, vol. 8, *Margaret Ogilvy*, p. 185.
2. Ibid., pp. 164–165.
3. Ibid., p. 166.
4. Ibid.
5. Personal communication.
6. Barrie, *Works*, vol. 4, *Tommy and Grizel*, pp. 417–418.
7. Ibid., p. 505.
8. Denis Mackail, *Barrie: The Story of J. M. B.*, p. 225.
9. Barrie, *Works*, vol. 4, *Sentimental Tommy*, p. 8.
10. Barrie, *Works*, vol. 4, *Tommy and Grizel*, p. 154.
11. Ibid., pp. 164–165.
12. Eventually these stories were published — first as a part of Barrie's novel *The Little White Bird* (1902) and later separately, as *Peter Pan in Kensington Gardens* (1906).
13. The story of Barrie's relationship with the Davies family is told at length in Andrew Birkin's excellent book, *J. M. Barrie and the Lost Boys*.
14. See Patricia Merivale, *Pan, the Goat-God; His Myth in Modern Times* (Cambridge: Harvard University Press, 1969).
15. Barrie, *The Plays of J. M. Barrie*, p. 27.
16. Ibid.
17. Barrie, *Works*, vol. 8, *Margaret Ogilvy*, p. 173.
18. Barrie, *Works*, vol. 1, *Peter and Wendy*, p. 225.
19. Barrie, *Plays*, p. 30.
20. Ibid., p. 85.
21. Quoted in Birkin, *J. M. Barrie and the Lost Boys*, p. 155.

22. Janet Dunbar, *J. M. Barrie: The Man Behind the Image,* p. 328.
23. Ibid., p. 326.
24. Barrie, *Plays,* p. 607.
25. Harry M. Geduld, *Sir James M. Barrie,* p. 163.

11 / HAPPY ENDINGS: FRANCES HODGSON BURNETT (pp. 136–143)

1. Ann Thwaite, *Waiting for the Party,* p. 30.
2. Ibid., p. 33.
3. Ibid., p. 37.
4. Ibid.
5. Ibid., p. 74.
6. Frances Hodgson Burnett, *Little Lord Fauntleroy,* p. 38.
7. Thwaite, *Waiting for the Party,* pp. 75–76.
8. Burnett, *The Secret Garden,* p. 1.
9. Ibid., pp. 6–7.
10. Ibid., p. 161.
11. Ibid., p. 162.

12 / BACK TO POOH CORNER: A. A. MILNE (pp. 144–155)

1. "House on Pooh Corner," sung by Kenny Loggins on *Sittin' In* by Kenny Loggins with Jim Messina, Columbia Records. I am grateful to my student Laurence Bassoff for calling this album to my attention.
2. Roger Sale, with characteristic daring, was the first American to break this silence, in "Child Reading and Man Reading: Oz, Babar, and Pooh," *Children's Literature,* vol. 1 (1972).
3. Frederick C. Crews, *The Pooh Perplex: A Freshman Casebook,* pp. 141–142.
4. A. A. Milne, *Autobiography,* p. 286. (For Christopher Robin's own version of his childhood, see Christopher Milne, *The Enchanted Places.*)
5. Ibid., p. 40.
6. Ibid., p. 38.

7. Milne, *Winnie-the-Pooh,* p. 43.

8. Milne, *Autobiography,* pp. 37–38.

9. Ibid., p. 35.

10. Ibid., p. 21.

11. Ibid., pp. 53–55.

12. Milne, *The House at Pooh Corner,* p. 56.

13. Ibid., p. 58.

14. Milne, *Winnie-the-Pooh,* p. 90.

15. Milne, *The House at Pooh Corner,* p. 66.

16. Milne, *Winnie-the-Pooh,* p. 45.

17. Milne, *Autobiography,* p. 229.

18. Ibid., p. 230.

19. Ibid., p. 9.

20. Milne, *Winnie-the-Pooh,* p. 69.

21. Ibid., pp. 120–121.

22. Ibid., pp. 7–8.

23. Ibid., p. 41.

24. Milne, *By Way of Introduction,* p. 59.

25. Milne, *Autobiography,* p. 19.

26. Milne, *By Way of Introduction,* p. 32.

27. Milne, *Autobiography,* p. 107.

28. Milne, *The House at Pooh Corner,* pp. 175–176.

29. Ibid., p. 84.

30. Ibid., p. 87.

13 / HEROES FOR OUR TIME:
J.R.R. TOLKIEN AND T. H. WHITE (pp. 156–168)

1. Parts of *The Book of Merlyn,* however, were incorporated
into books I and IV of *The Once and Future King.* For a
complete discussion of the changes White made, see Martin Kellman's *T. H. White and the Matter of Britain.*

2. Sylvia Townsend Warner, Prologue to White, *The Book
of Merlyn,* p. ix.

3. Warner, *T. H. White,* p. 28.

4. Ibid., p. 310.

5. Ibid., p. 210.

6. Ibid., p. 213.

7. Ibid., p. 97.

8. Ibid., p. 23.
9. Warner, Prologue to White, *The Book of Merlyn*, p. ix.
10. White, *The Book of Merlyn*, p. xiii.
11. Ibid., p. xvi.
12. Ibid., p. 61.
13. Ibid., p. xiv.
14. Ibid., p. 90.
15. Ibid., p. 129.
16. Ibid., p. 11.

14 / THE POWER OF SMOKEY:
RICHARD ADAMS (pp. 169–177)

1. Much of Adams's information was drawn from R. M. Lockley's *The Private Life of the Rabbit* (London: A. Deutsch, 1964), which as a result of his recommendation experienced a tremendous spurt in sales.
2. Adams, *Shardik*, pp. 19–20.
3. Ibid., p. 88.
4. Ibid., p. 232.
5. Ibid., p. 5.

15 / GAMES OF DARK:
WILLIAM MAYNE (pp. 178–188)

1. Margaret Meek, *The School Librarian*, March 1968.
2. Charles Sarland, "Chorister Quartet," *Signal*, September 1975.
3. William Mayne, *A Game of Dark*, p. 42.
4. Mayne, *Salt River Times*, p. 103.
5. Mayne, *The Yellow Airplane*, p. 15.
6. Mayne, *Max's Dream*, p. 27.
7. Mayne, *Salt River Times*, p. 160.
8. Mayne, *A Parcel of Trees*, p. 27.
9. Mayne, *While the Bells Ring*, p. 70.
10. Mayne, *Earthfasts*, pp. 17–18.
11. Mayne, *Winter Quarters*, p. 90.
12. Ibid., pp. 84–85.
13. Ibid., p. 111.

14. Ibid., p. 113.
15. Mayne, *A Game of Dark,* pp. 124–125.
16. Ibid., p. 34.
17. Ibid., pp. 74–75.
18. Ibid., p. 69.
19. Ibid., p. 95.
20. Ibid., p. 107.
21. Ibid., p. 7.
22. Ibid., p. 94.
23. Ibid., p. 11.
24. Ibid., p. 27.
25. Ibid., p. 59.
26. Ibid., p. 109.
27. Ibid., p. 133.
28. Ibid., p. 64.
29. Ibid., p. 133.
30. Ibid., p. 132.
31. Ibid., p. 141.
32. Ibid., p. 142.
33. Ibid.
34. Ibid., p. 143.

16 / THE FOLKLORE OF CHILDHOOD (pp. 189–204)

1. Iona and Peter Opie, *The Singing Game,* p. 64.
2. Ibid., p. 175.
3. Ibid.
4. Ibid., p. 78.
5. Ibid., p. 243.
6. L. P. Hartley, *The Travelling Grave and Other Stories,* p. 17.
7. Francelia Butler, *Skipping Around the World: The Ritual Nature of Folk Rhymes,* p. 178.
8. Ibid., pp. 83–84.
9. This and all following rhymes and jokes that lack citation are from my own collection.
10. Simon J. Bronner, *American Children's Folklore,* p. 76.
11. Francelia Butler, *Skipping Around the World,* p. 86.
12. Martha Wolfenstein, *Children's Humor,* p. 64.

Bibliography

Adams, Richard. *Shardik*. London: Allen Lane, 1974.

———. *Watership Down*. London: Rex Collins, 1972.

Alcott, Louisa. *Little Women*. Boston: Roberts Brothers, 1868.

Arrowsmith, Nancy, and George Moorse. *A Field Guide to the Little People*. New York: Hill and Wang, 1977.

Barrie, James. *Peter and Wendy*. London: Hodder & Stoughton, 1911.

———. *Peter Pan in Kensington Gardens*. London: Hodder & Stoughton, 1906.

———. *The Plays of J. M. Barrie*. New York: Scribner's, 1928.

———. *The Works of J. M. Barrie*. London: Hodder & Stoughton, 1913.

Baum, L. Frank. *The Wonderful Wizard of Oz*. Chicago: Geo. M. Hill, 1900.

Bettelheim, Bruno. *The Uses of Enchantment*. New York: Knopf, 1976.

Birkin, Andrew. *J. M. Barrie and the Lost Boys*. London: Constable, 1979.

Blair, James. *Mark Twain and Huck Finn*. Berkeley: University of California Press, 1960.

Bottigheimer, Ruth B. *Grimms' Bad Girls and Bold Boys: The Moral and Social Vision of the Tales*. New Haven, Conn.: Yale University Press, 1987.

Bremond, Claude. "The Morphology of the French Fairy Tale: The Ethical Model," in *Patterns in Oral Literature*, eds. Heda Jason and Dimitri Segal. The Hague: Mouton de Gruyter, 1977.

Briggs, Julia. *A Woman of Passion: The Life of E. Nesbit*. London: Century Hutchinson, 1987.

Briggs, Katharine. *The Anatomy of Puck*. London: Routledge and Kegan Paul, 1959.

———. *A Dictionary of British Folk Tales in the English Language*. Bloomington: Indiana University Press, 1970–71.

———. *An Encyclopedia of Fairies: Hobgoblins, Brownies, Bogies and Other Supernatural Creatures*. New York: Pantheon, 1976.

———. *The Vanishing People: Fairy Lore and Legends*. New York: Pantheon, 1978.

Bronner, Simon J. *American Children's Folklore*. Little Rock, Ark.: August House, 1988.

Browning, Robert. *The Pied Piper of Hamelin*. Illustrated by Kate Greenaway. London: George Routledge, 1888.

Burnett, Frances Hodgson. *Little Lord Fauntleroy*. New York: Scribner's, 1886.

———. *The Secret Garden*. New York: Frederick A. Stokes, 1911.

Burnett, Vivian. *The Romantick Lady*. New York: Scribner's, 1927.

Butler, Francelia. *Skipping Around the World: The Ritual Nature of Folk Rhymes*. Hamden, Conn.: Library Professional Publications, 1989.

Carroll, Lewis. *Alice's Adventures in Wonderland*. London: Macmillan, 1866.

———. *Through the Looking-Glass, and What Alice Found There*. London: Macmillan, 1872.

Clifford, Lucy Lane. *Anyhow Stories, Moral and Otherwise*. London: Macmillan, 1882.

———. *Aunt Anne*. New York: Harpers, 1892.

———. "Wooden Tony," in *The Last Touches*. London: A. & C. Black, 1892.

Crews, Frederick C. *The Pooh Perplex: A Freshman Casebook*. New York: Dutton, 1963.

Dunbar, Janet. *J. M. Barrie: The Man Behind the Image*. Boston: Houghton Mifflin, 1970.

Ellis, John M. *One Fairy Story Too Many: The Brothers Grimm and Their Tales*. Chicago: University of Chicago Press, 1983.

Engen, Rodney. *Kate Greenaway: A Biography*. New York: Schocken Books, 1981.

Fitzgerald, F. Scott. *Tender Is the Night*. New York: Scribner's, 1934.

Ford, Ford Madox. *The Brown Owl, A Fairy Story,* by Ford H. Madox Hueffer, with two illustrations by F. Madox Brown. London: T. Fisher Unwin, 1892. Published as vol. 1 of The Children's Library. *The Brown Owl* was reprinted as *The Brown Owl: A Fairy Tale,* illustrated by Grambs Miller. New York: George Braziller, 1966.

———. *Christina's Fairy Book,* by Ford Madox Hueffer. London: Alston Rivers, 1906. It was reprinted as *Christina's Fairy Book,* by Ford Madox Ford, illustrated by Jennetta Vise. London: Latimer House, 1949.

———. *The Feather,* by Ford H. Madox Hueffer, with frontispiece by F. Madox Brown. London: T. Fisher Unwin, 1892. Published as vol. 10 of The Children's Library.

———. *Memories and Impressions.* London: Chapman & Hall, 1911.

———. *The Queen Who Flew, A Fairy Tale,* by Ford Huffer, with a frontispiece by Sir E. Burne-Jones. London: Bliss, Sands, & Foster, 1894. *The Queen Who Flew* was reprinted in 1965 by George Braziller, New York, with illustrations by Grambs Miller.

Froud, Brian, and Alan Lee. *Faeries.* New York: Abrams, 1978.

Geduld, Harry M. *Sir James M. Barrie.* New York: Twayne, 1971.

Grahame, Kenneth. *The Wind in the Willows.* New York: Scribner's, 1908.

Green, Roger Lancelyn. *Fifty Years of Peter Pan.* London: Peter Davies, 1954.

Greenaway, Kate. *A Apple Pie.* London: George Routledge, 1886.

Grimm, Jacob and Wilhelm. *The Juniper Tree and Other Tales from Grimm,* selected by Lore Segal and Maurice Sendak. New York: Farrar, Straus and Giroux, 1973.

Hartley, L. P. *The Travelling Grave and Other Stories.* London: James Barrie, 1951.

Harvey, David Dow. *Ford Madox Ford, 1873–1939, Bibliography of Works and Criticism.* Princeton, N.J.: Princeton University Press, 1962.

Hoff, Benjamin. *The Tao of Pooh.* New York: Dutton, 1982.

Huygen, Wil. *Gnomes.* New York: Abrams, 1977.

Jason, Heda, and Dimitri Segal, eds. *Patterns in Oral Literature.* The Hague: Mouton de Gruyter, 1977.

Keightley, Thomas. *The World Guide to Gnomes, Fairies, Elves, and Other Little People.* New York: Avenel Books, 1978.

Kellman, Martin. *T. H. White and the Matter of Britain: A Literary Overview.* Lewiston, N.Y.: Edwin Mellen Press, 1988.

Lane, Margaret. *The Tale of Beatrix Potter,* rev. ed. London: Frederick Warne, 1968.

Laski, Marghanita. *Mrs. Ewing, Mrs. Molesworth, and Mrs. Hodgson Burnett.* London: Arthur Barker, 1950.

Leaf, Munro. *The Story of Ferdinand.* New York: Viking, 1936.

Lear, Edward. *Nonsense Songs, Stories, Botany, and Alphabets.* London: Bush, 1871.

Littlefield, Henry M. "The Wizard of Oz: Parable on Populism." *American Quarterly,* Spring 1964.

MacDonald, George. *The Princess and Curdie.* London: Chatto and Windus, 1883.

McGlathery, James M., ed. *The Brothers Grimm and Folktale.* Champaign: University of Illinois Press, 1988.

Mackail, Denis. *Barrie: The Story of J. M. B.* New York: Scribner's, 1941.

Mayne, William. *Earthfasts.* London: Hamish Hamilton, 1966.

———. *A Game of Dark.* London: Hamish Hamilton, 1971.

———. *Max's Dream.* London: Greenwillow, 1977.

———. *A Parcel of Trees.* London: Penguin Books, 1963.

———. *Salt River Times.* London: Hamish Hamilton, 1980.

———. *Underground Alley.* Oxford: Oxford University Press, 1958.

———. *Winter Quarters.* London: Cape, 1982.

———. *While the Bells Ring.* London: Hamish Hamilton, 1979.

———. *The Yellow Airplane.* London: Hamish Hamilton, 1968.

Milne, A. A. *Autobiography.* New York: Dutton, 1939.

———. *By Way of Introduction.* New York: Dutton, 1929.

———. *The House at Pooh Corner.* New York: Dutton, 1928.

———. *Winnie-the-Pooh.* New York: Dutton, 1926.

Milne, Christopher. *The Enchanted Places.* New York: Dutton, 1975.

Mitchell, Lucy Sprague. *The Here and Now Story Book.* New York: Dutton, 1921.

Mizener, Arthur. *The Saddest Story, A Biography of Ford Madox Ford.* New York: World Publications, 1971.

Moore, Doris Langley. *E. Nesbit: A Biography*. London: Ernest Benn, 1933; rev. ed. 1967.

Nesbit, E. *The Book of Dragons*. London and New York: Harper & Bros., 1899.

——. *The Enchanted Castle*. London: T. Fisher Unwin, 1907.

——. *Five Children and It*. London: T. Fisher Unwin, 1902.

——. *Five of Us, and Madeline*. London: T. Fisher Unwin, 1925.

——. *Harding's Luck*. London: T. Fisher Unwin, 1909.

——. *The House of Arden*. London: T. Fisher Unwin, 1908.

——. *The Magic World*. London: T. Fisher Unwin, 1912.

——. *The New Treasure Seekers*. London: T. Fisher Unwin, 1904.

——. *Nine Unlikely Tales*. London: T. Fisher Unwin, 1901.

——. *The Phoenix and the Carpet*. London: George Newnes, 1904.

——. *The Railway Children*. London: Wells, Gardner, Darton, 1906.

——. *The Story of the Amulet*. London: T. Fisher Unwin, 1906.

——. *The Story of the Treasure Seekers*. London: T. Fisher Unwin, 1899.

——. *The Wouldbegoods*. London: T. Fisher Unwin, 1901.

Opie, Iona, and Peter Opie. *The Oxford Dictionary of Nursery Rhymes*. Oxford: Oxford University Press, 1951.

——. *The Singing Game*. Oxford: Oxford University Press, 1985.

Potter, Beatrix. *The Journal of Beatrix Potter*. London: Frederick Warne, 1966.

——. *The Tale of Peter Rabbit*. London: Frederick Warne, 1901.

——. *The Tale of Pigling Bland*. London: Frederick Warne, 1913.

——. *The Tale of Two Bad Mice*. London: Frederick Warne, 1904.

Rahn, Suzanne. "Tailpiece: The Tale of Two Bad Mice," *Children's Literature*, vol. 12 (1984): 78–91.

Roth, Philip. *Portnoy's Complaint*. New York: Random House, 1969.

Sale, Roger. "Child Reading and Man Reading: Oz, Babar, and Pooh," *Children's Literature*, vol. 1 (1972): 162–172.

——. *Fairy Tales and After*. Cambridge: Harvard University Press, 1978.

Schreiber, Georges. *Portraits and Self-Portraits*. Boston: Houghton Mifflin, 1936.

Seuss, Dr. *The Cat in the Hat*. New York: Random House, 1957.

Soskice, Juliet M. *Chapters from Childhood*. London: Selwyn & Blount, 1921.

Spielmann, M. H., and G. S. Layard. *Kate Greenaway*. London: A. & C. Black, 1905.

Thwaite, Ann. *Waiting for the Party*. New York: Scribner's, 1974.

Tolkien, J.R.R. *Tree and Leaf*. London: George Allen & Unwin, 1964.

Travers, P. L. *Mary Poppins Comes Back*. New York: Reynal and Hitchcock, 1935.

Twain, Mark. *The Adventures of Tom Sawyer*. Hartford: American Publishing, 1876.

Updike, John. *The Coup*. New York: Knopf, 1978.

——. *Of the Farm*. New York: Knopf, 1965.

Warner, Sylvia Townsend. *T. H. White*. New York: Viking Press, 1967.

Weiss, Timothy. *Fairy Tale and Romance in the Works of Ford Madox Ford*. Lanham, Md.: University Press of America, 1984.

White, T. H. *The Book of Merlyn*. Austin: University of Texas Press, 1977.

——. *The Once and Future King*. New York: Putnam, 1958.

Wolfenstein, Martha. *Children's Humor*. Glencoe, Ill.: The Free Press, 1954.

Zipes, Jack. *The Trials and Tribulations of Little Red Riding Hood*. South Hadley, Mass.: Bergin and Garvey, 1983.

Index